The Historic Faith

and a Changing World

The Historic Faith
and a Changing World

BY W. NORMAN PITTENGER, S.T.D.

General Theological Seminary, New York

148314

GREENWOOD PRESS, PUBLISHERS
WESTPORT, CONNECTICUT

In gratitude and with deep affection
TO HUGHELL FOSBROKE
for thirty years Dean of the General Theological Seminary.

His firm faith and hospitable mind taught those who studied
under him that orthodoxy and sound learning, conviction
and a questing spirit, loyalty to the Church and loyalty to
the truth, are necessary in this as in every age.

Preface

The title and the table of contents explain sufficiently the purpose of this volume. It is an attempt to survey the contemporary American scene, both culturally and from a more specifically 'political' point of view, and in the light of that study to consider the relevance of Christianity to the emerging society. In order to do this the writer has been obliged to make certain assumptions, to read 'the signs of the times' in a way that seems right to him but may seem wrong to others. This is obvious and unavoidable. Surely one must have some *stance* from which to attack the problem.

It is also obvious that the particular religious convictions of the writer have to some degree—perhaps to a very large degree—molded his writing. He is an Episcopalian; as an Episcopalian, he is (as he would phrase it) a Catholic of the Anglican obedience. But he has earnestly sought to write in such a fashion that whatever is said may have its relevance to any understanding of historic Christianity; and what is said critically of particular positions is said because he thinks that these involve certain *mis*understandings of historic Christianity that are harmful or dangerous or both.

Because it is hoped that a wide public may read these pages, they have not been loaded with references and notes—always an effective way of putting off the general reader. It is necessary, therefore, to make here in the preface a blanket acknowledgment of indebtedness not to a score but to hundreds of other writers, to countless books, to conversations and discussions, to fellow-teachers and students. The dedicatory note expresses the writer's first debt—owed to one who has been a never-failing friend, a kindly but relentless critic, and a teacher as great as this country can ever hope to know. Dr. T. S. K. Scott-Craig, Professor of Philosophy in Dartmouth College, has been particularly kind in discussing with the author many of the ideas presented in this book.

It should be noted that the words 'liberalism' and 'orthodoxy' have been placed within quotation marks when reference is being made to contemporary or near-contemporary movements of thought or 'schools.' When the words are used without quotation marks, the usual dictionary sense is intended. In the case of the word 'orthodoxy,' it was especially necessary to follow this usage, since one of the main contentions of the book is that the contemporary movement known by that name is not always orthodox in the traditional Christian sense.

W. Norman Pittenger

Rumson, New Jersey, 1950

Contents

The Historic Faith

and a Changing World

1] *Introduction*

Several years ago, during one of the darker periods in the recent war, the writer of these pages was invited to make the principal address at a great gathering of clergy representing a large geographical area and including persons of many diverse points of view. The topic assigned to him was 'The Answer of the Church to the World's Crisis.' In order to discuss this subject at all adequately, it was necessary to give a preliminary survey of the crisis to which the Church's answer was directed, and to do this as honestly and objectively as possible. But when the address was finished and the time for questioning came along, the speaker was astounded and dismayed to find that his analysis of the crisis was discussed and criticized not on the basis of its accuracy or in relation to the concrete facts, but solely on the grounds of whether or not those who took part liked or did not like the picture. One person remarked, 'Do you mean to say that you want such-and-such to happen in our world?' To which the reply could only be made: 'What I like or dislike is not in question; the question

3

at issue is simply whether the "signs of the times" point or do not point in this direction.'

The fact is that one of the saddest failures of many Christians today is their unwillingness to see that wishful thinking is both dangerous and absurd. Of course this fallacy is not confined to Christians; it is well-nigh universal. Yet it ought surely to be the peculiar duty of those who are committed to the God who is Truth to look as honestly and objectively as they can at the truth, whatever it may be; our Christian faith ought to deliver us, at least partially, from the tendency to interpret solely in terms of our own desires and predilections. It may very well be that one hates with all one's soul the way things are or the way they are going to be; yet one must accept the fact as it is or as it will be and try to adjust one's thinking to it. 'Things . . . are what they are, and the consequences of them will be what they will be; why then should we desire to be deceived?' So the great Bishop Butler enquired; and even if we cannot help but wish them otherwise, we can at least recognize the error of the popular song of a few years back, which idiotically affirmed, 'Wishing will make it so.' It won't; and we are only being fools if we persist in 'fooling ourselves.'

Now all of this is said because the changing cultural scene of our time, visible to our eyes, is so plain that it ought to be accepted for what it is, even if we do not happen to like what we see; whereas the shape of things to come, while not inevitably of the pattern herein sketched, is in the writer's judgment almost certainly so. In other words, one of the first steps toward an understanding of the place Christianity can occupy, must oc-

cupy, in the emerging society with its new cultural outlook, is an honest recognition of the facts. Otherwise,
the discussion will be utterly irrelevant to the actual
state of affairs—as, alas, Christianity has seemed to be
to so many for so long.

There is, of course, no reason under the sun why the
Christian faith should be *adjusted* to the new pattern
of things; in fact, if the attempt is made to do so, in the
obvious sense of complete accommodation, the integrity
of Christianity will be denied and its claim to be a
judgment upon the world will be abrogated. One of the
worst evils of the now much-decried 'liberal era' in religious thought was found precisely at this point. If
Christianity were not being adapted to the thinking of
the *laissez-faire* capitalistic world, it was being adapted
to the newer optimistically conceived liberalistic world.
If it did not serve as a means for condoning the evils of
an 'acquisitive society,' it served as a dynamic for pro-
ducing a 'socialized society.' In either case, the wholeness, independence, and self-identity of Christianity
were minimized or lost.

On the other hand, it would be wrong to think that
since Christianity cannot be accommodated to a given
society or culture, it has no relationship to it and is in
no way influenced by the good and sound achievements
of that society or culture. An illustration of this violent
reaction, as we shall see, is the way in which the 'new
orthodoxy' of our own age has rejected, sometimes in a
cavalier manner, the enormous contribution that 'liberalism' made to Christianity—in the development of
Biblical criticism, the easing of the problem of religion's

relation to science, the newer understanding of the relation of faith and fact, the recovery of the historic Jesus as the necessary complement to the Christ of orthodox faith. Doubtless 'liberalism' was unfortunate in most of its emphases and in many of its conclusions; doubtless it reflected the 'spirit of the age' and influenced Christianity too much in that direction. But to make a simple and total refutation is wrong. And, it may also be hinted, the 'new orthodoxy'—with its dogmatic affirmations (made sometimes quite apart from any reasoned argument), its occasional neo-fundamentalism in regard to Holy Scripture, its contempt for human reason as so vitiated by sin that it is thoroughly untrustworthy—is not without its hidden affinities with the irrationalism and political dogmatism of our own contemporary age. Better far to have some sort of open and acknowledged relation to the society or culture in which Christianity exists, even if that be a relation marked by tension and trial-error, than to have either a complete separation on the one hand or a subtle and unrecognized reflection of secular ideas and forces on the other.

The truth is that the word 'tension,' used in the preceding sentence, is the key to our understanding of the right relationship between Christian faith and secular culture. A 'tension' is like a rubber-band; sometimes it is stretched so vigorously that it becomes strained and taut, while at others it is held loosely so that it is relaxed and easy. The double 'dialectic' is found here: first, between culture and Christianity; secondly, between one moment or kind of relationship which is sharply critical or strained and another moment or kind of relationship which is more relaxed and genial. Both are necessary, and one without the other becomes almost demonic in its false claims and its exclusive assertions.

But to return to our earlier consideration of Christianity's apparent irrelevance to the contemporary cultural scene. 'Apparent' is indeed the wrong word, for the painful but inescapable truth is that Christianity really does not make much (if any) difference in our culture today. In the next chapter we shall discuss this culture at some length, attempting to analyze its dominant trends and characterize its main assumptions. But even at this point we must make clear that these trends and assumptions are certainly not specifically or consciously *Christian,* in any real and significant sense.

When the Christian bodies of America, through their several agencies such as the national organization of Roman Catholic bishops, the conferences held under the auspices of the Federal Council of Churches of Christ, the conventions, assemblies and other gatherings of denominational leaders, express their opinion of great national or international issues, they do unquestionably have a certain influence. But the influence is one that arises not from the essential *rightness* of their position, as it is seen to *be* right by governmental or other agencies, but rather from the fact that the pronouncements may possibly represent a weight of votes or a potential pressure upon officialdom. Furthermore, as is not often enough seen, the various pronouncements —on labor problems, for example, or on international

issues of all kinds—come from a select number of denominational leaders or Christian spokesmen, and do
not accurately indicate the real state of mind of the
'church' constituency. One can say that a number of
well-known and thoughtful citizens, who are deeply
Christian in conviction, have agreed to certain ideas,
and that these ideas have been expressed in public with
some clarity. The possibility is that they may, to a
greater or lesser degree, win the imagination of many
voters and, by influencing their attitude toward those
in authority, compel the 'rulers' to take the pronouncements into account. It cannot really be claimed, with
any semblance of accuracy, that the specifically Christian point of view or specifically Christian assumptions
have much to do with governing national or international policy.

Again, in the matter of personal morality we have an
illustration of the irrelevance of the Christian view to
the contemporary scene. The assumptions upon which
the sexual life of young America is based could hardly
be called specifically Christian—and the author says this
without wishing for a moment to be puritanical or negative in his attitude toward sexual expression. Our army
and navy chaplains during the last war saw clearly that
since Christianity had not deeply penetrated the inner
lives of the youth of our land, forming in them 'a Christian mind,' the only method by which they could combat promiscuity and its lamentable consequences was,
on the whole, the 'army' way—warnings of physical ills,
admonitions to strengthen morale, and provision of
prophylactic and precautionary means of avoiding un-

desirable results. Even among sincerely Christian young people, the assumptions underlying their sexual life are not always—one might even say, not often—consciously Christian. That their 'pastors and masters' are at fault is obvious; but the facts are obvious, too. The sexual *mores* of America are not genuinely Christian in any impressive manner.

It may very well be felt that this picture is far too somber. Things are not so bad as they are here represented; it may be said: the writer sees only 'the dark side' and there are many brighter considerations that might be adduced. Of course there are brighter considerations, and of course the dark side is being emphasized. But is it not a fact that while there are brighter considerations, some of which we shall discuss in later chapters, the dark side is the more potent and effective and dominant today? Is it not precisely a sign of our tendency to 'kid ourselves' that we seek always 'the silver lining' rather than honestly face the darkness? If we find a 'silver lining,' do we not arrive at it only when we have first known that darkness? Thomas Hardy's remark, 'If way to the better there be, it exacts a full look at the worst,' is pertinent here. The writer would say that it is part of his total Christian orientation to believe that he *must* have this sort of 'provisional pessimism,' as George Tyrrell called it, before he dares to have, with Tyrrell, an 'ultimate optimism.'

There was a time, not too long since, when Christian assumptions were consciously or unconsciously dominant and determinative in western society. Of course men and women 'sinned' then, as they do now—that is to be expected of the 'sons of Adam.' But they were aware of the fact that they 'sinned.' By this we mean that the actual assumptions consciously held about human life, its purpose, setting, meaning, and dignity, were Christian assumptions; or, if they were not consciously held, they had so permeated the sociological and psychological milieu that they served (so to say) as archetypal patterns for behavior. Therefore when men and women 'did that which was wrong'—or, in other words, when they acted in a way that did not agree with the assumptions—they knew they were departing, wilfully or in some other fashion, from the accepted standards. This is not so today.

In the first place, the practical assumptions that govern life are very different—as we shall see presently. In the second place, one of the assumptions, which we might call *the assumption behind the assumptions,* is that the over-all guide for living is expediency or, as it could be termed, 'the pragmatic sanction.' In a slang phrase, 'anything goes'—if you can 'get away' with it; or, from another side, 'for those who like this sort of thing, this is the sort of thing they will like.' Hence the very *notion* of a dominant and determinative set of assumptions is, in effect, regarded as outworn and even stupid. A misuse of the relativity principle is often provided as the intellectual justification for this rejection of assumptions that shall govern life. It is odd that this should be done—or perhaps it is an indication of the general misapplication of a truth from one sphere; for, as anybody who has some acquaintance with the newer physics is aware, the whole point of the relativity principle is that it is a provision for that adjustment in calculation which shall make possible an absolute determination. That is what Einstein was seeking; that is what he, with other specialists, believes he has found— a correction in observational error which will make accurate statement in given fields attainable.

Furthermore, a perversion of the principle of toleration has been at work in our minds. The sheer fact that 'the world is so full of a number of things' has led to the conclusion that every one of these things is equally good and sound and true. From that conclusion has come the consequence that since some like one thing and others like another thing, anything and everything is right and valuable; the only difference between one thing and another is that John likes this and Frank likes that. Such a sanction can lead only to chaos—as indeed it has led. It is not necessary to assert that any one of us, or all of us together, can know with utter certainty and clarity *the* absolute; it is necessary, if only for intelligible discourse, to assert that we must judge at least in terms of *approximations* to the absolute. Above all, it is necessary that we should have the humility and the common sense to recognize that people born before, say, 1900 or 1910 were not entire fools—that is to say, that the past can teach us much about what is good and sound and true, even if its teaching must always be checked and rechecked in the light of our own experience and thought. Failure to understand and admit this has wrought havoc in our world, because it has destroyed, or at least minimized, the idea of generally accepted assumptions that can govern our life and our actions.

Perhaps this is as it should be—at least, it may be inevitable and necessary that Christianity, as 'the City of God' in *earnest* or as the first fruits of that City in the present world, which is at best 'the city of man,' cannot again be the heart and center of what M. Maritain (in his magnificent book *True Humanism*) has called a 'sacral' civilization; perhaps it ought never to have consented to be such, even in the Middle Ages. But the fact is plain, no matter what the 'ought' may be. And we must take account of that fact, seeing it for what it is and dealing faithfully with it.

Let us put it quite bluntly. Even among those who 'profess and call themselves Christians'—and by this mean what they say—there is a strong tendency to succumb at some point or other, or at many points, to the influence of a predominantly non-Christian culture. This patent dilution of Christian 'ideas' by other assumptions may indicate a necessary strategy for the Church in the future; to that problem we shall give attention later on. But whatever the Church's strategy may be, the situation to which organized Christianity addresses itself must be faced realistically. V. A. Demant and others have said that we are living in a 'post-Christian' era; they mean that Christianity as a dominant and determinative force has lost its power over the contemporary world, having been succeeded by a point of view which, however indebted to bits of Christianity that persist like flies in amber, is in its over-all nature un-Christian. The situation is all the more tragic because many do not even recognize it to be so. We do not suggest that the intellectual leaders, who to a considerable extent are responsible, are themselves unaware of what has happened—too frequently, indeed, they desire precisely what they have accomplished. Marx and Freud, for example, were not Christians by any stretch of the imagination; what they say that *is* 'Christian' is said, as it were, by accident rather than by deliberate intention. Those who have followed in their train have been even more certainly enemies of Christianity. Go through a list of the really formative minds of the past quarter-century and consider how many of them are 'post-Christians.' Many philosophers, critics, novelists, poets, scientists of all descriptions, can be put in this category. If this were not so, we should hardly be in the somewhat comic position of rejoicing when a great name, like that of T. S. Eliot or W. H. Auden among the poets, Sir Arthur Eddington or Sir James Jeans, among the scientists—to mention only a few typical figures—definitely identifies himself with the Christian faith and writes and speaks from that faith. Those who are confident of the general acceptance of a given position are usually not so exultant as we tend to be when a distinguished man gives his assent to the position. They take the position 'for granted.'

We may be happy that Christianity is no longer taken 'for granted.' If the Christian position is believed today, it is believed—rather more often than yesterday—because it is felt to be *true*, not because it is the 'atmosphere' that one naturally accepts in a given cultural situation. And yet something is lost, surely, when common assumptions about life and human destiny no longer exist, or, if they do exist, are at the poles from the whole and integral Christian ones. What is it that is lost? In a word, it is the presence of some universe of thought and norm of action, which makes *sense* of our culture. This certainly is true if there are *no* assumptions. If the assumptions that are accepted are not Christian, what is then lost is a common acceptance of a setting for life and a guide for action that sees man in his 'misery and grandeur' as the sinning yet redeemable child of a living God, whose loving-kindness gives a dignity and even a sublimity to human life and whose saving action for man makes man a 'gentleman' with the possibility of becoming a 'saint.' He would be a most perverted or blind observer who did not regard the loss of this common assumption as a very grave loss indeed. Even Mr. Middleton Murry, in his non-Christian days, saw this: 'There is no God,' he wrote, 'and we cannot *live* without him.'

Our concern in this study is primarily with the American scene—a world survey is far too ambitious an undertaking for us to attempt. The references we may make to other countries and to their cultural and political problems will be in a way incidental, although not entirely so, since we live now in a world that certainly must be seen as 'one world,' to use Mr. Wendell Willkie's famous phrase. Even the best efforts of some of our political leaders on both sides of the water to turn 'one world' into 'two worlds' and to foment strife between those two—an effort that is doubtless unintentional on their part but that surely appears to be the inevitable result of their talking and their actions—cannot undo the simple fact that by reason of our economic interdependence, our planetary interrelatedness, and our social and cultural interpenetration we are all bound together 'in one bundle of life.' But our interest in this book is the way in which all this impinges on and makes changes in our American situation. If America is our subject, we must acknowledge that, to a very large degree, the loss of many common assumptions and the substitution of non-Christian or dubiously Christian assumptions for those that were definitely derived from the Christian faith have been a 'sea-change.' The shift within the past twenty-five to forty years has been enormous. For America was not only founded and developed by men who were fundamentally Christian—if not with the fullest and heartiest personal conviction, then at least by reason of their genuine acceptance of Christian ideas—but it was also a country in which the fashion of thought and the standard of action for over a hundred years were consciously molded on what were conceived to be Christian 'ideals.'

We must admit frankly—and later discussion will attempt to demonstrate—that much of this American thinking and many of these American 'ideals' represented a profound misunderstanding of Christianity and a serious misreading of the facts about human nature and the world. The falsely optimistic world view, the perfectionist theory of human nature, the inheritance of Lockean notions concerning substance that led directly to political 'spiritualism' at the expense of denying man's inherent 'materiality,' the individualism (also inherited from Locke, as Dr. Northrop has shown in *The Meeting of East and West*) that negated man's social 'conditionedness'—all these, and more, were mistaken and in the end may prove disastrous to the whole American 'experiment' if they are not corrected in time. Even if we grant this, we must still affirm that the general assumptions about life and human destiny that went into the total American scheme and guided its development were Christian in essence. No matter how interpreted, the assumptions included the being of God, the operation of his will in history (has there ever been a more profound understanding of this than in the thought of Abraham Lincoln?), the place of man as his creature, the fact that man is a sinner but that he has dignity and nobility, the 'hope of glory' in a fulfilment beyond death—here, indeed, are Christian assumptions. When men like Henry Adams came to disbelieve in these assumptions, they had the wit to see and the honesty to assert that they were in effect destroying the basis of American life, whether they rejoiced in the fact or regarded it as a necessary but horrible accomplishment.

One can only wonder, then, that so few Christians in this land—including discerning thinkers of the Christian Church—have taken sufficient account of this fact. We have heard lamentations about the lowered moral standard, and we have heard the sad admission that church attendance has dropped off badly during the past thirty years or so. But apart from men like Reinhold Niebuhr and other prophets of our generation, there has been far too little grasp of the total cultural change and far too little recognition of the necessity, in view of this change, for a reorientation of Christianity to the national life. Our church people, by and large, have simply gone on their way; and two world wars, with their concomitant depressions and disturbances, do not seem to have shaken them very much. At certain recent conferences, attended largely by laymen, the predominant opinions were two: one was the simple belief that all is well, that the Church is doing nicely, and that American life is in a sound and healthy state; the other was that while much is sadly amiss about our situation at home, not to speak of that abroad, the solution is fairly simple—the 'acceptance of the Christian religion' by everybody and the application of 'Christian principles' to our problems. The last-mentioned idea— that 'Christian principles' should be applied—is doubtless admirable and unquestionably valid, if one knows just what 'Christian principles' are and how they are to be applied. But it is here that we come once again to our fundamental difficulty: it is a change in our cultural scene, with all that goes into it, that confronts us and that demands such new techniques and such modifications in Christian attitudes and aptitudes as are anything but simple. To face this fully and honestly would mean that the laymen who were in attendance at the conferences mentioned above would be forced to listen to those 'gloomy Jeremiahs,' like Dr. Niebuhr, who see the darkness and are not inclined to stress 'the silver lining.' It would mean that the laymen would be forced to agree that, since the assumptions by which American life is governed are so vastly changed from those which were effectual at the end of the last century and the early years of this one, things are very different indeed, and that we are confronted by a 'new order' that requires both the courage to see and the capacity to undertake an almost total readjustment of outlook and a thoroughgoing reappraisal of the relation of Christianity to society.

If a clergyman may say it without offense, it must be noted that on the whole the ministry is much more aware of what has happened and is happening than are the laity. Not long ago, at a discussion in connection with the meetings of a ministerial association, the writer came to realize this very clearly. It was not that the ministers—of all denominations—were worried about their church attendance or financial support; on the whole, these seemed to be good enough. It was rather that they sensed a profound gulf between their understanding of the Christian 'mind' and the 'mind' of the communities in which they worked; even in their own congregations they felt that there was present a kind of phenomenon called by modern depth-psychologists 'schizophrenic.' Church people really suffer from split personalities; one-half of them is loyally given to the Christian faith and its implications, while the other half is formed and guided by secular thinking and acting. This fact has expressed itself not only in the usual 'Sunday religion, Monday business' dichotomy—that might merely be the conventional failure to carry into all areas of one's public life the professions of one's private conviction. Neither is it that Christians fail, both in personal and in social action, to measure up to their profession—that is simply the reflection of the sinful nature of man. Nor is it that the pattern of human life is so complicated and intricately adjusted that even the best intentions fail of realization—that is the dilemma of 'moral man and immoral society.' The *real* schizophrenia is within the very soul of the Christian himself; his final loyalties are divided, so that in the innermost depths of his being he is torn between conflicting assumptions about life and the meaning of life.

Schizophrenia is the expression of exactly the problem with which we have been concerned. It is so deep-seated, often so hidden, that the 'pious layman'—and frequently enough, too, the consecrated pastor or priest —does not even recognize it, would deny its presence, or would laugh at its supposed pervasive power. But this is Plato's 'lie in the soul'—so far down, so terribly real but so dreadfully disguised, that it possesses a potency entirely unsuspected and therefore utterly uncontrolled. Demant, to whom we have already referred, has made the distinction between what he describes as the 'dogmas' and the 'doctrines' of our age; by this he means that there are in our culture unconscious beliefs and motivations (so hidden that they are not recognized) that govern our lives, while with our conscious minds and our conscious wills, we profess quite different, and perhaps contradictory, beliefs and motivations. Surely he has touched with a needle's point the chief ailment of our time; it is our cultural-religious schizophrenia.

The contemporary world, then, is neurotic, as Karen Horney has told us. But the Christian theological scene itself is confused. 'Liberalism' is dead, at least in the seminaries, among the leaders of thought, and among the younger ministers. 'Orthodoxy' is on the way in; on every hand we see evidence of a return to something like the historic faith of the ages. To this subject we shall devote considerable attention in a succeeding chapter, for it involves much that is relevant to our total problem. But the immediate and practical result of the return of 'orthodoxy' is a certain bewilderment and confusion in the Christian Church itself. In retreating from the widely accepted 'reductionist' Christianity of the pre-war period, the danger is that the Church may 'throw away the baby with the bath water.' We have already mentioned certain aspects of this danger, but there is another phase requiring our attention.

Dr. Paul Tillich, in the course of some private discussion about the German theological situation during the period between the wars, stated as his own firm conviction that the 'neo-orthodoxy' of Karl Barth and his disciples was largely responsible for the withdrawal of German youth from the Church. This was due to the fact that Barth insisted that the revelation of God in his Word 'cut across' human life and experience to the extent of virtually denying to that life and experience any true significance. He taught that all that men do, however they do it, is sinful and must be negated by God's Word. Barth was forced by events to change his view and to speak vigorously for a Christian attack on the evils of Nazism, but only after the damage had been done. German youth, which might have been won to a genuinely humane Christianity, turned instead to a demonic religion that at least sanctified 'blood and soil' and gave high meaning to the immediacies of every-day life in the Germany of the 'thirties.

The recovery of 'orthodoxy' has its danger, right at the point we have been discussing. If it should mean what has been called an 'extricationist' view of religion, in which 'salvation' from the world is the only consideration, it will leave the field open for the un-Christian or partially Christian assumption, to which we have referred, to win an open victory. In this sense, at least, our contemporary schizophrenia is better than a complete integration around a false or misleading world view. It is indeed here that the balance in historic Christianity between the dogmas of the Incarnation and the Atonement is so valuable; for the assertion of Christian faith is that God not only saved man, through Christ, *from* the confusions and contradictions of life in this world, but that he did it *in* this world and in the midst of those very confusions and contradictions. That is, he gave significance to every aspect of human life and experience, redeeming the mundane immediacies so that they were directly related to and found their full value guaranteed by the ultimate dependabilities which subsist in the very structure of things. In a phrase, God made life safe at the center and meaningful at every point on the periphery.

Finally, we must see, the only solution of our problem that can do justice to all the terms is one that leaves man in the position in which it finds him, at least to the extent of leaving him with problems that are not completely soluble but that must be met as they arise. A genuine solution must not deny any of the terms in order to arrive at an easy answer. Nor must it pretend to have any final and all-inclusive answer; God became incarnate not to make it unnecessary for us to use our brains, but to give us the power to use them well and wisely, without the perversion of thinking that sin introduces into our minds. Thus it remains true that man is a citizen of two worlds. He lives in the realm of the finite and the temporal; he is limited and conditioned by circumstance and event. At the same time he lives in the realm of the absolute and the eternal. This is true for non-religious men as much as for religious ones. It is a given fact of our existence, as is also the tension that results from this double-belonging. We cannot escape it; we must accept it and make what we can out of it.

But the unique contribution that Christianity can bring to our changing culture and our emerging social order is an insight into the true nature of our eternal home, and with that an insight into the true relation between that abiding reality and the flux and flow of temporal and finite existence. It is for want of these insights that we perish. And perish we do. For the appalling truth is that on the one hand the common assumptions of our culture deny the reality of our eternal destiny; while on the other, the assumptions by which we live are predicated on an even deeper falsehood—namely, that human life has *no* significance or meaning beyond expediency and the 'pragmatic sanction.' Mr. Justice Holmes illustrates precisely this point; his only final standard, as he confessed to Sir Frederick Pollock, was one of workability—and, in the end, he had to admit that this meant that power, in however sublimated a sense, was the final determiner of truth and hence of justice.

If ever there were a division in the center of personality, it was here. Justice Holmes was a liberal and humane man, whose 'dissenting opinions' were almost invariably on the side of 'the common man'; yet his own assumptions contradicted his generous 'opinions.' On the other hand, if our Christian faith is regarded as one concerned solely with 'the other world,' we are in as sorry a case. For then, as we have seen, we can at best 'extricate' ourselves—or be extricated by some downthrust from above—from 'this untoward generation.' That step would leave the world thoroughly unredeemed.

It is, then, the duality of our citizenship that we must accept; and, as Christians, we must use our insights—which themselves spring from 'the truths of revelation,' as William Temple taught us to see—to build up a set of assumptions about life and human destiny that are, for us at least, dominant and determinative. This action will mean a sharpening of the difference between secular society and the Christian position; it must *not* mean a complete separation of the two, after the fashion of Karl Barth in Germany between the wars. Even while our supreme loyalty is to 'the City of God' and our assumptions are those that spring from that allegiance, we must live in the world under the conditions of temporal confinement and spatial limitation; we must be members of a mundane society with its complications and intricacies; we must function as men in the midst of the flux and flow that unite us, on our bodily side, with the world of material change and movement.

But, it must be asked, what is the actual cultural situation? What are the assumptions, conscious or unconscious, to which we have so often referred? What is the general pattern of American life? It is to this many-faceted question that we shall address ourselves in the next chapter.

2] *The Changed Cultural Scene*

Not very much discernment is required, on the part of those of us who are over forty, to see that things in America are not what they used to be when we were adolescents. And if we take a longer perspective, it is only too plain that the old *mores,* by which life in our land was governed, have nearly disappeared, and have been replaced by a new set of *mores* that bear little, if any, resemblance to what were the accepted ideas and habits fifty years or more ago. How the change has occurred, what are its explanations, does not at the moment concern us. We are engaged in the task of discovering, if we can, the assumptions that are either implicit or explicit in our cultural scene—as they might, for example, strike the visitor from another planet or even from another and quite different civilization.

The first and most obvious fact about the picture is simply its sameness. Uniformity is the keynote of the American scene—of that there can be no doubt. A few years ago, the writer drove across the United States by automobile. From New York City through New Jersey and Pennsylvania, he traveled through the southern states, missing only one or two of them en route. A swing through the Southwest included Arkansas, Oklahoma, Texas, New Mexico, Arizona, Utah, Nevada, and California. The journey proceeded up the Pacific coast to Seattle and into western Canada, east by way of the northern states to the Great Lakes, and back to New York after a visit to New England. In all, thirty-one states and a distance of some fourteen thousand miles were covered.

The trip provided a magnificent opportunity to observe the general cultural scene in America—and, in this context, to see plainly the fact that the scene is uniform. There is no *fundamental* difference, culturally speaking, between Maine and California, between New York City and Seattle, between the Northeast and the Northwest, the Southeast and the Southwest. Of course there are tremendous differences not only in scenery and setting but in dominant trades and industries; there is great variety in the architecture and the planning of cities and towns. There is a remarkable contrast between the rather suspicious attitude toward strangers in the eastern states and the geniality and hospitality shown in the western states.

But it must be insisted that these are relatively *superficial* differences. Beneath them, there is a sameness reaching almost to the point of sheer monotony. The Midwest, for example, may be more isolationist in its outlook than the Far West or the East Coast, and even the presence of countless veterans does not appear to have modified that outlook. But the things in which the people are interested, the subjects about which they talk and to which they constantly return, the axioms from which they argue, and above all the common assumptions about life and destiny that they hold, are the same. It is not merely that the people of America dress in the same kind of clothes and use the same colorful slang (which changes from year to year, month to month, yet somehow seems to sweep the country); it is not merely that they drive the same kind of cars and eat the same standardized food products. Fundamentally, it is that they like the same kind of things and accept the same kind of values and assume the same kind of ideas—*given* ideas—about 'what matters most.'

To a considerable degree, no doubt, the material and physical sameness in clothes, food, cars, standards of living, and so on, is the carrier for the 'spiritual' sameness; but whatever the fact may be in regard to the *how* of it, the *that* of it is inescapable. Conversation with a garage-hand in Prescott, Arizona, did not reveal any essential difference in 'outlook on life' from that of a pleasant and helpful chance acquaintance in a little town in northern Montana; and neither of these seemed to have points of view or assumptions that contrasted with the ideas implicit in the talk of a Vermont 'tourist-camp' manager. No attempt was made to 'pump' these people; the conversation was always on the ordinary level of familiar give-and-take; 'high thinking' was not in question. The important thing was the fact that the discerning mind could read, behind the words and the exchange of somewhat superficial ideas, the underlying 'philosophy,' so to speak, of the three men.

Nor was it different when the opportunity was afforded to talk with men and women of the 'intellectual classes.' At dinner parties, over cocktails, in informal chatter late at night, perhaps after a concert in the San Diego outdoor amphitheatre, or with—of all things!—an educator in New England, the uniformity of outlook was the striking thing; and behind that uniformity of outlook was an almost complete uniformity of basic assumptions, taken for granted and unquestioned.

But what are the elements in that uniformity? What, in fine, are the common assumptions that lie behind our cultural identity? They would appear to be reducible, roughly, to the following: (1) Expediency or, as we have called it earlier, the 'pragmatic sanction' is the fundamental rule for action. (2) Absolute or universal truths are unknowable, hence what may be termed 'relativism' is the only possible 'way.' (3) 'All men are created equal,' which means that they have equal talents and capacities. (4) *Things* are the essential realities; therefore spiritual 'realities' of every sort, in art and literature as well as in religion, are according to taste or attraction, and in any case are secondary to the hard 'facts,' even if in some sense they may sometimes be said to have a kind of 'ideal' priority. (5) Self-expression to the degree of complete self-fulfilment in the present world is possible and is the right of every man.

These assumptions are part and parcel of an optimism and a bland perfectionism that are inherent in contemporary culture. The world war has not destroyed them, nor have depression and suffering had any effect. For a while, it may have been hoped that the pessimism, the complete hopelessness and the sense of frustration so widespread in Europe, would have some effect not only on our intellectuals, but on all life this side of the Atlantic; this does not seem to have occurred. We did not suffer sufficiently; and the *typical* American still entertains the belief that with a certain amount of 'gadgeteering,' a reasonable degree of manipulation, a better grasp of the requisite techniques, we shall be able to get on the straight road to perfection once again. American optimism is unquestionably a legacy of the 'frontier spirit,' as Dr. Turner long ago pointed out; perfectionism is tied up with the 'liberal' spirit that so long pervaded our life. Both have flourished due to the vast room for expansion in a relatively new continent; and the mingling of many races in one great 'melting-pot' has meant that great numbers of hitherto 'underprivileged' persons have had advantages and opportunities denied them elsewhere. In a religious dress and in certain temporal situations, optimism and perfectionism have a degree of justification; but they have become 'articles of faith' in America, but of a faith that is without genuine religious insight and is in contradiction to the concrete facts. They continue as part of the American pattern of life.

The first of our common assumptions is that whatever 'works' is true and good. This notion is plainly linked with the next assumption, which we have characterized as 'relativism,' yet it is somewhat different and may be considered separately. The typical American, in considering any course of action that is proposed to him or any line of thought that may attract his attention, is

not likely to indulge in long speculation about what
he should or should not do, believe or disbelieve. He
has a handy test he can apply, and he applies it in-
stantly. The test is simply: how far is this thing practical, workable, likely to succeed? It is no accident that
the philosophy of 'pragmatism' comes to us from Peirce
and James, two American philosophers, nor that its
development into instrumentalism has been the work
of a third American, Dewey. Nor is it an accident that
Dewey contends in his *Quest for Certainty* that there
is no reality antecedent to the business of acting, of
doing, of working. The notion that there should be appeal to some static, or supposedly static, reality or principle or standard is not at all sympathetic to the average
American, especially the American of the present day;
he wants 'results,' and he will judge in terms of what
is likely to get 'results.' The writer has even heard this
point of view given scriptural vindication through the
use of the text, 'By their fruits ye shall know them'—
surely a misuse of scripture if ever there were one! The
American's assumption is not that grand one of Baron
von Hügel, who used to insist that *one* of the ways by
which truth was proved was its long-range, many-sided
'fruitfulness.' That, surely, is closer to the scriptural
idea and is entirely valid and sound. But our common
American assumption is different; it is the belief that
tangible, almost immediate, workability is what we
must go by.

Business, presumably, must be conducted largely on
this basis; and since American culture is vastly governed
by 'business' considerations, it is perhaps natural that

similar notions should permeate the national life. The 'hard-headed' businessman, whose concern is with what he is pleased to call 'facts,' represents one kind of pragmatist; the engineer, or the man with the machine, represents another—in each case, it is his job to make things run, to make them run so well that there is increase in what is called 'efficiency.' This 'efficiency' is the corollary of the 'pragmatic sanction.' Doing more things more quickly is regarded by most Americans as equivalent to doing them well; at least, that is the impression we tend to give. This is linked with our emphasis on the machine, the gadget, the device. Never has there been such an overwhelming consciousness of the implement or the tool as is found in America; we are worshippers of the 'machine.' An American youth can handle intricate tools, engines, and mechanical appliances with a skill and facility that astound foreigners; and this technical competence is one of the sure signs of 'Americanism.' Wherever it is found, there American ideas have spread, be it in darkest Africa or in remotest China. It is all part and parcel of the assumption that workability—and by implication, the *best* kind of workability—is the test for almost everything. Even when Americans are concerned with quite different matters— as, for example, church unity—they 'operate' (in itself a significant word) on this principle. The author cannot forget his bewilderment at hearing a distinguished theologian insist on the immediate union of two Christian bodies of quite disparate theologies and polities, on the single ground that they could work more effectively together, with more efficient administration and results commensurate with the effort expended.

We have mentioned that the second assumption is closely related to the first. That second assumption we have called, roughly enough, the notion of 'relativism.' By and large, Americans are sure that while there *may* be some absolute and eternal truth, it is not to be got at—or at least, not to be got at very easily. Hence, for all practical purposes—and, as we have indicated, practical purposes are what matter, according to the first great assumption—we must accept a quite general 'relativity.' Every idea is taken to be as good as every other idea, except that more people may hold one idea than another. This has its good fruit, to be sure. Toleration of minorities, on the whole, is an American virtue—although in recent years it has been somewhat hard pressed, with the growth of an un-American anti-Semitism and racial prejudice. But the kind of tolerance that all too often has sprung from the feeling that absolutes are unreachable is what we may call a 'tolerance of indifferentism.' 'Anything goes,' provided somebody believes in it. And if he believes in it *sincerely*, then it is 'all right for him.'

This element of sincerity is essential for the American. Indeed, one of the highest compliments we can pay someone is to call him 'sincere.' Once the writer ventured to remark, after this compliment had been paid a distinguished but (as he thought) misguided leader, 'So is the devil!' The joke was not much appreciated, for its point simply did not get across to the auditor. But sincerity is surely a good thing, as a quality of personality. With insistence on sincerity goes a similar insistence on what may best be denominated by the old slang term, 'solid.' To call a man 'solid' meant to say that he had integrity; it meant that he believed what he said and practiced what he believed. This, like sincerity, is a splendid and commendable quality—and one of the fine things about American life is its admiration for men and women who are persons of integrity. But it does not go very far unless one is sure of that for which such persons stand—and if the assumption is that almost anything is 'all right' if it is not socially outrageous, then there can be no very definite meaning attached to what in effect is only a good attitude.

The third assumption is concerned with the equality of men. As this belief was historically held by the 'fathers' of our country it did not mean, apparently, what it is taken to mean today. They said that 'all men are created equal'—that is, they are equal in that they are all creatures, made by God and treated 'equally,' or with perfect justice, by him; hence they meant that no constraints that were unfair or unjust should be imposed upon any man. Presumably it did not imply what Americans today assume, that 'every little boy or girl that's born into the world alive' can become an Einstein or a Horowitz, or some other remarkable genius, if he or she is given the proper education and not denied rightful opportunities.

Older cultures have always maintained, in one form or another, the need for recognition of 'diversities of gifts'; we in America are not happy about this idea; we fear the implications of what seems an 'aristocratic' principle. For some time, the educational system of the country was based upon the 'aristocratic' idea of training leaders; then it went over to the implementation of the sound precept of 'equality of privilege,' but carried it to an extreme that refused any recognition of special capacities and qualities. Where education is at the moment is anyone's guess; but one can easily see, in the hysterical attacks on the movement toward a revival of the liberal-arts college, that great numbers of Americans are ready with the assumption that human *equality* means human *identity*. We must hasten to add, lest there be serious misunderstanding at this point, that we do not for a moment wish to suggest that the several races, religions, colors, and so on, are unequal in any sense demanded by a genuinely democratic recognition of humanity's solidarity, nor do we deny the 'rights of every man' to as full an education and to every other advantage, including economic and social privilege, as may be humanly possible for him. The point that we are making is quite different; it concerns only the common American assumption that the right to be treated justly rests on an *identity* of human ability. It is possible, indeed, that this assumption is not unrelated to the idea that men are all part of a great mass, without any 'individual' in Kierkegaard's sense; yet that idea would hardly do justice to the inveterate individualism of the American mind, even if it should have support in the uniformity that a national press, radio, the motion pictures, and other forces have tended to stimulate or even to inculcate.

When we turn to the fourth of the assumptions, we

have come pretty close to the heart of the American cultural scene. For *things* are respected in America to an amazing degree. On the very day of writing, a young man remarked to the writer that he (the young man) was much more interested in *things* than in people or ideas; perhaps he exaggerated, but since he said it quite spontaneously and (blessed word!) 'sincerely,' there must have been at least an element of truth in it. While we do read books and see plays and hear concerts, we love most of all to drive cars and run machines; we think in terms of *things,* if only in the sense that we are vastly interested in quantity, in numbers, in measurement, in statistics. Reference has already been made to our devotion to 'gadgets' and mechanical tinkerings; the avocations of our youth seem to run increasingly to this sort of amusement, rather than to broader 'cultural' interests. Music on the radio is more popular than learning to play an instrument; the radio itself is both a symptom and an augmenting of the *thing*-worship in our midst.

The corollary of this is that what we have called 'spiritual realities' are given a secondary place. They are for those who like them and according to the taste of the likers. This means that here again there is a recurrence of 'relativism'; even more obvious is a dismissal of any and every traditional standard of judgment. The wisdom of the ages is not too highly valued in America, on any count; in 'spiritual matters' it is seldom even taken into consideration. Hence our religious fads; hence our espousal of silly 'causes,' lost or otherwise; hence our taking up with new and eccentric schools of art or music; hence our peculiar interest in so-called 'realistic' and sometimes morbid literature, to the exclusion of the higher realism that can see somewhat above the ephemeral and can get out of the gutter in order to understand the significance of that gutter.

The fifth and final assumption is that men should express themselves, that they have the right and the capacity to achieve that self-expression to the limit and in this world. Now if men were in fact capable of complete self-fulfilment, they ought to be given the chance to express themselves fully so that they can achieve their proper end; and, in any event, nothing *unnecessary* ought to be put in the way of any man, at any time, doing his utmost to 'be himself.' So much we should and must grant. But we in America seem to assume a kind of infinite self-empowered development toward a complete mental, bodily, and (in our own way) spiritual selfhood as a genuine and entirely realizable possibility for men. Interference with this is regarded as wicked; it is here that our individualism comes directly to the front. The ancient sense of the impotence of man, his sinfulness and essential finitude, does not play a large part in American thought. We assume that man is good, that he can become perfect, and that anybody who, or anything which, gets in his way is by that token bad.

Now that we have insisted on these basic assumptions in the American scene, we must at once go on to admit that we have been unfair. The presentation has been 'loaded' on the negative side; it has been far from adequate; there are many considerations that more or less balance one or other of the points we have made.

And yet, even with this frank admission of unfairness, we believe that what has been said is the 'larger half' of the truth. This, something like this, some variant of this, does in fact lie behind our cultural scene. Consciously or unconsciously, we do make these assumptions.

One illustration of a balancing consideration may be given. Americans are individualists; yet they are also deeply 'social-conscious,' as the phrase has it. Of course this may only be part of a desire to 'keep up with the Joneses,' but it may be deeper and more genuine. Americans 'like to get together'; they are gregarious by nature and they have a good time when they are part of a group. Furthermore, they have developed a certain real interest in social welfare; they are concerned for the good of society, even if that concern manifests itself only in contributions to 'community chests.' So in our picture of the American scene, we ought not to forget the other side of the picture. But it is so easy, and so dangerous, to pick out the good points and forget the bad— easier, really, than to pick out the bad ones and forget the good. And our American optimism makes us peculiarly prone to do the former; the present study is a conscious attempt to see the latter—that is, the bad points—without completely perverting the total picure.

Nor must it be forgotten that in each of the assumptions there is something that is genuinely good and sound. The trouble is that the good is embedded in or expressed by something that is fallacious or so partially true that it tends to put the sound elements in a false perspective and destroy the right proportion of things.

This is regrettable; all the more regrettable because it need not be so. The vitality, the vigor, the attractiveness of much in our American scene is vitiated by false perspective and disproportion—and it is this that makes it fundamentally tragic, so that one is inclined more to weep than to scoff.

A further element widespread in our culture, and yet hardly to be classed among the assumptions, must be mentioned before we turn to other questions. It is the common feeling that 'anything is all right if you can get away with it.' One could hardly link this with any of the previous five points, although it comes fairly close to several of them, and particularly to our 'pragmatism' and 'relativism.' A simple illustration is the attitude of children in certain areas of New York City, who were reprimanded for stealing small articles from large five-and-ten-cent stores. They could see no moral question here; it was simply a problem of whether or not they could take what they wished, without being observed in doing so. Or again, the increasing prevalence of 'cheating' in examinations, which has led schools and colleges that formerly had depended upon the so-called 'honor system' to return to the custom of proctoring the examination halls. Or again, the remark made in the writer's hearing by a quite excellent young person, who, when asked how it was possible to take on an extra job that, if it were known, would automatically remove the right to a war-service pension, replied: 'Oh, nobody will find out.'

Our illustrations have been drawn from the younger generation but this common notion is not confined to them. It has governed a considerable amount of business operation and industrial enterprise—to put it mildly; it is found in almost every area of our national life, personal and social. But it is certainly most clearly shown in the youth of the land, as proved by reports of activity in the army and the navy. Yet the armed services, while they doubtless contributed to this widespread idea, were not the originators of it. The real cause is the collapse of any widely accepted set of moral standards, and this is coincident with the collapse of the permeating and pervasive influence of Christian assumptions on the population.

The fact is that the 'what you can get away with' idea is not so much the absence of *any* moral standard as it is the substitution of another idea of morality for the old one. The youthful American is not entirely lacking in morality; on the contrary, he is a very moral being in two senses of that word. In the first place, he is a *conformist,* as we indicated in our emphasis on the uniformity of the American pattern; in the second place, he has an idea of morality that is essentially new. The rules are to be elastic enough to permit him to have his own way in emergencies or when particular needs and desires come to the fore. It is obvious that this kind of morality is anything but sound, according to objective standards; the point is that many Americans do not even understand what you are talking about when you say this. The reason for this misunderstanding once again illustrates our thesis about the common assumptions of our culture.

For if expediency and 'relativism' are considered as

rules, so to say, they lead to exactly this state of affairs; the result is that there are *no* rules excepting the one that judges by what a person 'can get away with.' Hence it is impossible to appeal to any accepted principle that may be taken as final. The reply will simply be, 'I don't see it.' And that is that—further argument or discussion is impossible, unless prudential grounds can be adduced as a deterrent to the particular action that is under discussion.

This is shown perfectly in the attitude taken toward sexual relationships. We shall speak of this at some length later; here we can make our point sufficiently plain by reference to a question that is difficult to handle adequately in a book of this sort: namely, the matter of homosexuality. Doubtless in the past there has been a stupid misunderstanding of the homosexual, with failure to recognize his situation and take sufficient account of the physiological, psychological, and sociological factors that enter into it. In any event, the attitude taken in the past has been one based on a principle, although that principle was neither very clearly stated nor thought through very satisfactorily.

Today we are told there is a tremendous increase in homosexuality among both sexes, aggravated by the war but reflecting other aspects of a disordered and neurotic age. We may be grateful that the attitude now taken about this mode of sexual expression is not nearly so much the disgust of an earlier day. We have outgrown our sense of horror; and this is all to the good—that attitude was no way to solve the problem or to help those who were involved in it. But unless the writer is mistaken, the prevalent attitude is one of 'it's all right for those who are built that way, but they mustn't make themselves social nuisances.' Since prudential grounds, in the ordinary meaning, cannot here be adduced for individuals, the appeal must be to assumptions stated earlier—pragmatism and relativism and their corollary in expediency. But surely, in such a matter, more should be said: if homosexuality is to be condoned, it must be on principle; if it is to be condemned, once again it must be on principle, and without prejudice to enlightened methods of dealing with it as a social phenomenon. Instead, we have a confusion of thought that does nothing more to solve the problem than the old-fashioned disgust. This question, like all fundamental moral questions, can soundly be considered only on the basis of assumptions in regard to the nature of man, his final destiny, and the order of things. On Christian assumptions, we should reach one set of conclusions; on present American assumptions, we can reach only a *laissez-faire* solution, coupled with social control that itself is based on grounds of expediency.

In a traditionally established culture, with a living religion at its core, there is one obvious fact, as Arnold Toynbee has shown in his *Study of History*. It is the enormous influence of faith over every aspect of the culture; nothing is said or thought, nothing is attempted or achieved, without some reference—be it explicit or implicit—to the dominant religious orientation. So it was in America, in an earlier day. But now that the 'acids of modernity,' in Mr. Walter Lippmann's phrase, have seemed to make religion (at least in its familiar

dress) incredible to many thinking men, and to those
who are not thinkers, has thrown a certain suspicious
dubiety over the accepted faith of our fathers, this can
no longer be said. The diffused effects of religious faith
are not so potent as once they were, if indeed they have
power at all. So what A. R. Vidler has termed 'general
Christianity,' as distinct from institutionally embodied
and firmly held 'specific Christianity,' has become so
dim and vague that we should have difficulty in describ-
ing it as much more than the smile that remains when
the Cheshire cat has disappeared.

However, in a survey of the American cultural scene,
we must not forget the presence of organized Christianity, with its churches and congregations all over the land.
Surely, one would think, it must make an enormous
contribution to the life of Americans. It does indeed
make a contribution. It would be ridiculous to minimize its weight and absurd to deny its influence. Even
today, when church-going and church membership are
not necessary to respectability and when it is on the
whole probably more conventional to be inactive in
church life (at least to the extent to which at one time
—barely a quarter-century ago—it was the conventional
thing), it is still true that organized religion plays its
part in the scene. An English visitor to America some
years back remarked with amazement at the way the
Church exerted influence here—but the influence he
observed was brought about by pressure groups and
official representation to national and state governing
bodies, rather than by the permeation of the whole life

of the land with definitely Christian standards and principles.

One of the most remarkable facts of our time is that the Church can exercise an influence in one direction when its influence in another direction seems very slight. Through its commissions and committees it can do much —as the group representing the non-Roman communions, at the San Francisco meeting to establish the United Nations, illustrated; yet it seems to do very little so far as the subtle and almost hidden springs of life and action in America are concerned. Let us not exaggerate this point; it is certainly true that a considerable number of Americans are still loyal to their particular church or denomination. To that loyalty they give much of their time, much of their interest, support, and allegiance. But what do they get out of it?

We do not mean this in a crude fashion, deserving of a rejoinder such as 'They get out of it what they put into it' or 'One doesn't become a churchman to get anything for oneself.' That is perfectly true. What we mean here is quite different. Our question is simply the degree to which the churchman's whole outlook on life, his assumptions and standards, are governed by the principles for which the Church stands, by what it teaches, by what is implied in its faith and expressed in its worship. Do the majority of Americans, even the most active church people, get *that* from their church affiliation?

A certain discrimination is necessary. The influence of the Church upon American culture has been largely by way of 'promoting' (if the horrid word may be used) a spirit of service, helpfulness, and idealism, which commends itself to many people. The activism of American life, to which we have already referred and to which we later shall revert, is expressed by this spirit, for Americans want to be doing something; hence, 'what a man does' is thought to speak louder than what he believes or assumes. This is one of the strange fallacies in American culture. Emerson long ago put the real truth in reverse fashion: 'What you *are* speaks louder than what you *say*,' and, we should add, 'than what you *do*.' The dominance of a religious outlook that is fundamentally *ethical* rather than dogmatic, *practical* rather than speculative, *activist* rather than devotional, is inevitable in an America whose whole cultural pattern is built either about business or 'busy-ness.'

In consequence, as we shall see when we examine the sphere of sexual morality, there is a gap between much professed belief and the 'believer's' genuine underlying assumption. It is a gap that is not consciously seen by those who are its victims, and it is an illustration of that schizophrenia described in the introductory chapter. American culture was largely 'formed,' in the old days, by Christian and religious considerations; today these considerations 'hang on' and certain of their atmospheric consequences, so to say, are still present also. But these Christian assumptions are not operative as dominant and determinative in our culture. We are obliged to conclude, sadly enough, that in so far as our previous analysis and discussion of the common assumptions of our American life has come anywhere near the mark, the Christian Church's influence is relatively slight in the total American scene.

The Church can be, and very plainly is, a dynamic for service and idealism, in some senses of those words; but on the other hand, it is adjectival to the life of the nation and the day-by-day living of its people. It does not provide the over-all pattern for the culture of the land—we do not have what M. Maritain calls a 'sacral' culture, nor do we have even a culture predominantly molded by Christian considerations regarding the nature of human life, its limitations and sinfulness, its need for redemption, its fundamental dignity as well as its tragic frustration, its destiny beyond this world. If T. S. Eliot is right in speaking of the possibility of a 'neutral' society, America is perhaps in that condition; yet it might be more accurate to say that it is in an even more negative situation than that, for a 'neutral' society presumably suggests one that does not have *any* formed assumptions or unconsciously held principles, whereas our society most certainly does have these—and they are either very tenuously Christian or simply not Christian at all.

It is hardly of great significance, therefore, that the number of professing churchmen in America is either keeping pace with the growth in population or somewhat exceeding it. This would indeed be a very important fact if it meant that such a proportion of the population were in truth permeated by the total Christian conception of life. It is even now an important fact in one respect—that Christianity is still a 'live option' for many Americans and that many feel it worthwhile to 'belong' to one of the organized Christian bodies. This is all to the good—for unless we mistakenly regard the Church as a 'museum for saints,' we shall gratefully see that it is best regarded as a 'hospital for sinners,' and that it is not without significance so long as it can give to its members some reminder of human dignity and of man's divine calling. But it is hardly significant in the wide cultural sense. The authors of books like *Middletown* have shown us that the weight of the Church is not strongly felt in the average American community; and the recent studies gathered in the second volume of the *Interseminary Series* indicate that labor unions, fraternal groups, and other organizations of the sort do for many just about what the Church does for its members. If the Christian Church's cultural influence is equal only to that of such secular bodies, it can hardly be said to mold the pattern of American life, nor can it be said to be doing very much even for its own members.

To some degree—and in certain respects a considerable one—the Church has conformed itself to the general pattern of American life. Its social activities, its 'parish house' life, its main emphasis on 'attitudes' and on 'goodwill,' its insistence on the virtue of tolerance, are not so much to be criticized as they are to be seen for what they are worth: they do not represent the unique contribution that organized religion might make to the national culture if it were doing its job in nurturing men and women in an integral Christian orientation to life. Church services that are really meetings to hear lectures on moral principles; the confusion of devotion to the Christian religion with support of democracy and Americanism; the kind of thing represented by a church bulletin that urged businessmen to 'support the Church because it makes honest business possible in your community'—these do not contribute very much to broaden and deepen the life of the nation. All they do is give that life a kind of religious sanction. In fact, the best comment on the whole situation is to be found in a delightful newspaper report of a large public gathering, in which, after an account of several 'important' speeches and the adoption of some plans for 'community betterment,' the reporter concluded: 'The Reverend So-and-so also spoke, adding a religious note.' Precisely: but if that is all it amounts to, it can hardly be said with any degree of confidence that the cultural pattern of America or its common assumptions are much affected by the presence of congregations of loyal Christians.

We revert to the matter of sex, this time in its aspect of heterosexual relationships, for illustration, since sexual *mores* are always an indication of the general cultural situation. Any analysis of the cultural scene in American today would record the astonishing development of 'sex-consciousness.' Subway advertisements, magazine pictures, even the weird comic books that represent a social phenomenon not yet adequately investigated, would be enough to convince us of this, even if we did not have the motion pictures and the stage, as well as the novels and short stories that flood the newsstands and book stores. Deeper than sexual expression is this consciousness of sex. It is not surprising that there should be a revulsion from puritanical standards, nor is it a wonder that two world wars, with the loosening of much that seemed firmly planted in the sexual *mores,* should have given rise to a change in outlook. What is significant about the 'sex-consciousness' of America today is its essential vulgarity. Let us consider this briefly.

Sex is an utterly central element in human life. As St. Augustine sixteen hundred years ago and Sigmund Freud yesterday ought to have taught us, if our own experience has not, man's personality is made for his fulfilment in an *other.* The physical and physiological, as well as the psychological and emotional, equipment of the human being is such that he inevitably seeks satisfaction in some love-object, from God, the *summum bonum,* to that which provides sheer gratification of physical desire. The problem of man, therefore, is the *right ordering* of this fundamental drive. When sex is vulgarized, it presents a strange and disproportionate appearance. The young man in love is plainly motivated by his sexual urges; but the romantic quality of his love, the 'idealism' surrounding it, the compulsion to sacrifice for the beloved, combine to give that sexual foundation a beautiful and ennobling dress, making the whole enterprise a fitting symbol even for the relation of the soul with God. When sex is presented and encouraged, without romance or 'idealism' or sacrifice, and when it becomes merely a means to cheap display or a way of pandering to uncontrolled fancy, then it has lost its beauty and nobility; it has been vulgarized in a nauseating fashion.

This cheapening of a great and wonderful thing has occurred in our American culture to a degree that is tragic and horrifying. And with this degradation has come a looseness in sexual expression that reflects precisely the same vulgarity. Much has been written about the increasing divorce rate, the ease of the long or short liaison, and the widespread promiscuity of our day. The substitution of amateur for professional prostitution, on a large scale, is a matter of simple fact, as newspaper statistics show. We need not repeat the sordid record. The point demanding our attention here is that all these are but ways of expressing a fundamental vulgarizing of the sexual life of man that is increasingly prevalent in our American society.

Let us take the matter at its simplest level. Anyone acquainted with the habits of American youth knows that 'necking' is part of the accepted *mores*. It is not even a moral problem or a moral issue for a vast number of the boys and girls, young men and young women, of the country. It is an expected and assumed part of a 'date' for the average American adolescent or young adult. The degree of intimacy allowed may vary enormously; the fact of it is taken for granted. It is far from the writer's purpose simply to decry this situation. Indeed, it is his judgment that as far as the Church is concerned a 'moral theology of necking' (to use a dreadful phrase) is demanded; the Church should never issue a flat prohibition of what has been called 'amorous play,' without some understanding and some sound casuistical handling of the question. Even so, the Church's standards, based as they are upon *Christian* assumptions concerning human life, simply do not matter to huge num-

bers of young people; even within the membership of
the Church, they have not counted for much, largely,
perhaps, because they have not been made more apparent. In any event, the fact is there. Once again, it is
a question of vulgarity. Intimate relationships are regrettable and wrong, even when there is love between
the couple but they are not planning for marriage on
its basis. But such sexual relationships have a crude-
ness, a cheapness, a vulgarity, about them if there is no
love at all between the parties, so that the relationship is
merely a means for gratification of an immediate or in-
duced sexual desire without the larger context in which
that desire must rightly be set if it is to be 'propor-
tionate.'

What we find lacking, then, in the American scene is
some balanced and ordered view of the sexual life of
man. What is substituted is simply another reflection of
one of the common assumptions to which we have already referred—namely, the assumption that it is perfectly proper 'to get what you can' without regard to
long-range consequences. This is the reason, presumably, that 'the vulcanization of rubber' and the perfect-
ing of other contraceptive methods and prophylactic
measures, have led to a tremendous increase in general
promiscuity. The old cautionary warnings do not hold
today. At least, if army and navy statistics are to be
trusted, they were not widely effective in the armed services although they were still the measures most frequently used to improve the sexual morality of service
units. If you can get what you want, and if what you
want is easily available, it requires a deeper set of as-

sumptions than the typical American ones to hold you in check: this is what it comes to.

As we have said, we have painted a picture that seems very dark. Yet we are bound to say that it seems to us true. But we must not forget, on the other hand, the happier features of the cultural scene. There is, to take another example, a surprising generosity in America. Appeals for help from institutions and agencies engaged in medical advance or the assistance of those who are ill will never go without a large response. There is kindness of heart in the average American; his apparent cynicism in some respects is accompanied by a splendid tenderness in others—it is proverbial that women and children are better treated in America than almost anywhere else. The American does not want to see a man 'down and out'; he will do anything in his power to aid such a person. It is possible to continue, at considerable length, to sketch this brighter side of the picture. But one cannot escape the feeling that it is not the *dominant* side, however widespread may be this fine idealism among our citizenry. Indeed idealism can even be a mask for an unconscious callousness that baldly expresses itself now and again in total indifference to the fate of other nations and peoples if only the latter will let us in America alone to enjoy our 'way of life.' And even that 'way of life' itself, while it has its fine qualities, is typically conceived of and generally portrayed in what for want of a better word we must call 'materialistic' terms; it is a matter more of *things* than of *being*, more of 'what we do' than of 'why we do it.'

The American himself is a person of 'charm.' He is

lovable, perhaps for his very naïveté. He has an adolescent curiosity, a capacity for unself-conscious behavior, for comradeship and bonhommie, which naturally make him delightful. But this delightful quality has its unfortunate side, because, like all adolescents, he is capable of a cruelty and a capacity for misunderstanding and impercipience that is often quite devastating. It might be said that to external observers the two characteristics most typically American are, on the one hand, likeability, and on the other, insensitivity.

This fact is not without significance, for it seems to spring from something akin to the common assumptions mentioned above. It is related to the heedless demand for action that we saw to be so integral to our whole culture. Depth of thought, genuine profundity of understanding rather than accumulation of statistics and that blessed thing called 'know-how,' seem to be sadly lacking even in men of intellectual prominence. They are qualities almost totally absent in our public leaders, as is apparent from the fumbling and amateur way in which serious economic, political, social, and international issues can be discussed in Congress, by our outstanding executives, and by 'experts' in our public forums. The belief that 'what we do' is the prime matter is so common that it is hardly necessary to remark upon it. To be active, to be 'up and doing,' to be 'on the job,' to be at work on something—this attitude is what Americans admire more than anything else. So we get a great deal accomplished, but frequently what is accomplished is without much value in the long run. We do not build for eternity; we build so that we may be busy doing something.

Along with this factor is a tremendous respect for 'organization.' The American may be an individualist; indeed he is that above all. But it would not be surprising to have him organize a society for the furtherance of individualism! In fact, it has already been done. This characteristic is admirably expressed in the story that three Americans who were shipwrecked at once proceeded to organize a committee, with chairman, vice-chairman, and secretary-treasurer; then they set out to develop a program. Even here there is a hidden conflict in the American mind. At the very moment that Americans talk 'big' about individualism and free private enterprise, they form associations such as the National Association of Manufacturers whose major interest is to protect monopolistic privilege. The supposed contradiction seems to escape their attention.

The great majority of us are unaware of the trend of society in our own day. That there is to be a planned and controlling state, either national or international or both, is known by our best thinkers to be inevitable. There are a few outstanding men and leaders in the political field who see this and are doing their best to make terms with the inevitable consequence of the pressure of events; but they are all too frequently rejected as 'crackpots' by the run-of-the-mill 'common-sense' American. And if they are 'experts,' they are almost sure to be dismissed as academic minds, out of touch with 'real' facts and hence 'talking through their hats.' So we seek to evade the truth by hiding our heads in the sand.

Another dominant element in our culture is a tremendous confidence in our own destiny—the future of the nation and its 'way of life.' This confidence is quite uncritical; it verges on a religious faith. Indeed, it *is* the American religion. Long ago, Professor Hayes described nationalism as 'the new religion.' He spoke of the scriptures of that religion—the writings of the 'Founding Fathers'; the saints—the great historical figures like Washington, Franklin, Jefferson, Lincoln; the rites—the national celebrations like the Fourth of July, Memorial Day, and Armistice Day exercises. He might have gone on to describe the heresies—all views that seem to criticize or question the accepted opinion about national greatness and destiny. He might also have mentioned the cultus in the schools, with the 'salute to the flag' and the 'pledge of allegiance.' All this comes very close to the heart of ordinary American life.

This kind of Americanism, which takes on an idealistic tinge and a vaguely spiritual air when it is the subject for orations and rhapsodic eulogies, has at its heart one specific religious quality: it demands from its believers their wholehearted devotion. Usually it gets it; even the somewhat jaundiced attitude of returning veterans has tended to evaporate so that the American Legion and similar organizations can once again represent the average citizen in his supreme loyalty to the 'national ideal.' The best expression of the American religion can go beyond this: it can be a dedication to certain social goals and moral ends, considered in a

very liberal and democratic spirit, such as is advocated
by Mr. John Dewey in his little book *A Common Faith.*

Yet underneath this, even underneath Mr. Dewey's
high statement, there remain the general assumptions
we have indicated. The supernatural, or any equivalent
of it, has dropped out of the picture; all the talk about
'values' and 'ideals' cannot conceal the absence of a
genuine faith that gives man more than a this-worldly
mundane significance. It is a 'workable' religion; it has
the quality of expediency; it insists on the primary importance of the *here and now;* 'relativism' is dominant
in its 'tolerance of indifferentism.' Above all, it maintains that man is good in nature; his mistaken actions
or perverse spirit are to be explained by either environ-
mental or heredity factors, which the right educational
techniques and the proper eugenic controls can satisfactorily modify. And it is implicit in the cult that
America is the place of, and loyal Americanism is the
means for, this amelioration.

In a word, the culture of America today lacks depth.
There is no adequate grasp of the seriousness of man's
condition; there is no real acceptance of his abiding sinfulness; there is little of the sense that his contemporary
dis-ease, which would readily be granted, is the expression of his fundamental disease, which would be denied
or minimized. We have our prophets—Reinhold Niebuhr, from the Christian side, is one; Lewis Mumford,
from a side that can hardly be properly described, is
another; yet when Mumford, for example, writes *The
Condition of Man,* faithfully, searchingly, profoundly
discussing our ills, his words are not given a real hear-

ing. Niebuhr is too much a Christian for the 'secular'
world to accept his religious views, although when he
writes in *The Nation* and elsewhere on the political
scene and on our mundane problems, he is heard with
respect.

It is at this very moment, and against this very scene,
that we are witnessing a revival of 'orthodox' Christian
conviction. It has come to us through a combination of
influences. First in the theological schools and now in
the active Christian ministry, it has become *the* new
thing in the Christian world. It would seem to speak in
flat opposition to the whole cultural scene in America.
So it does. But it has not yet been able to reach down
very profoundly into the pews or to shake the typical
lay confidence in the common assumptions of American
life, even among the faithful, much less to have any but
the slightest hearing among those who are completely
'unchurched.' To this recovery of 'orthodoxy' we shall
turn in our next two chapters, endeavoring both to interpret its main emphases and to consider the ways in
which it bears upon the cultural pattern of America at
large.

3] *The Recovery of 'Orthodoxy'*

Paul Elmer More used to relish a little tale about the new creed that, he said, was flourishing in New England among the 'liberal Christians.' This creed, as he quoted it, consisted of the following articles of belief: 'I believe in the fatherhood of God, the brotherhood of man, the leadership of Jesus, salvation by character, and the progress of the human race.' 'But,' he remarked, with a twinkle in his eye, 'I think a closing article should be added. It should conclude with the words, "and I believe in the neighborhood of Boston." '

Mr. More was not quite fair in confining the creed of American 'liberalism' to Boston and its environs; surely, even by the time he was telling with such delight this little story, the creed—without its Bostonian addition—represented the kind of thing prevalent throughout the American religious world. Probably very few people knew the precise words he quoted; yet in almost every denomination (including even some areas of Roman Catholicism) something like that creed was the real faith of great numbers of church people. In seminaries of all denominations, this kind of 'liberalism' was not only alive but flourishing—it was the new religion that was to supplant the older and supposedly outworn 'orthodoxies' of yesterday.

There were many factors to explain the rise of religious 'liberalism' in America. New England influence was one of these, certainly. From the beginning of the nineteenth century, in violent reaction from the strict Calvinism of the Puritans and their early American successors, a modified and liberalized version of the old theology had been sweeping the Congregational and later Unitarian pulpits. Emerson and the Transcendentalists, with their optimistic notion of man and their monistic view of the world, contributed their share. Later, students who went to Germany to study Biblical and theological subjects returned with the post-Kantian philosophy, the Ritschlian theology, and the Harnackian view of the essence of Christianity—this, of course, occurred toward the end of the last century and in the first years of the present one. Our natural American 'activism,' associated with our frontier mentality; the inevitable development of a theory of 'progress,' implied in the way in which the new land was 'up and coming,' with bigger (and presumably better) things ahead as year succeeded year; the sense of liberation from old fetters which resulted when men and women came to this country from the old world and found themselves almost entirely freed from tradition and custom, with the consequence that tradition and custom came to be regarded as outmoded and cramping—here

were some of the secular influences at work in produc-
ing 'liberalism' in religion.

Furthermore, the tremendous advance in scientific
study, especially in the field of biology after the days of
Darwin, made religious people uncomfortably aware
of the apparently restricted world view of the older
orthodoxy. They sought a way out, which in the end
meant that they simply adopted an evolutionary world
view and surrounded it with a kind of religious aura,
seeking to show not merely that there is no conflict between science and religion but that they are only different ways of saying the same thing—which was taken
to be a continuous progressive movement of the world,
and all that is in it, from lower to higher levels, with a
'far-off divine event' at the end in which a perfect social
order would be produced by the efforts of men inspired
by a 'power not ourselves that makes for righteousness.'

As the nineteenth century closed and the horrors of
industrialism became clearer, more sensitive souls began to react against the evils that grew out of the capitalistic economic system. To their delight, they found in
the Old Testament the writings of prophets like Amos,
and in the New Testament the Epistle of James. They
discovered that they could make a special reading of the
teaching of Jesus, after the miracles and the claims made
for his deity were ruled out as being later additions by
credulous believers, in which there was a 'social gospel'
that offered some religious justification for their social
conscience and for their demand that society should be
reformed.

Much else went into the religious melting pot which

in the end gave us the 'liberal' interpretation of Christianity. Here, it was believed, was a simple religion that in no way contradicted 'the modern mind'; a religion taught by the Hebrew prophets and lived out by 'the Galilean prophet'; a religion that refused to degrade man to the level of total depravity, but instead saw him emerging from the beast and moving on toward a golden age when peace, justice, liberty, and happiness would be enjoyed by all who dwelt on the face of the earth. With this world view a particular kind of theology came to be associated. It taught the fatherhood of God but minimized the omnipotence of God. It reinterpreted the divinity of Jesus to make it mean that he 'incarnated' the values men believed to be desirable; hence he could be the master of men and their leader in the battle for righteousness. But it said little about Jesus as the Saviour from sin in the traditional sense— since sin was only inadequate knowledge and imperfection of will which more education and better environment would remedy. This new theology shied away from 'the last things'—death, judgment, heaven and hell —because it was more concerned with making this world better than with preparing men for some hypothetical 'other world.' It regarded the Church as a society of pioneers in social reform and in the personal search for truth and goodness, while worship and sacrament were believed to be optional appendages, whose value was primarily in aiding men to live good lives and work for social improvement.

Of course these ideas were held with differing intensity by differing groups, but, in the main, something like this was the faith of American 'liberalism.' It appealed to the American mind, reacting as that mind does from supposedly old ideas, attracted always by 'something new.' It appeared to provide a religious sanction for the best and most idealistic American spirit. It offered an inspiration that, it was thought, could make this country truly the 'land of the free and the home of the brave.' Probably it is for this reason that it is still the religion spoken by our orators at patriotic meetings, at great rallies on July Fourth, and at memorial services on Decoration Day. It is, indeed, the kind of religion that is natural to those who identify the 'American way of life' with Christianity.

It would be a fascinating study to investigate the ways in which this 'liberalized' religion played its part both in preparing for and in underwriting those common assumptions of American culture to which we devoted the last chapter. In combination with many other influences and agencies, it had much to do with the whole shift in American mentality. But the extraordinary thing is that despite the fact that 'liberalism' was to a large degree responsible for the new assumptions, those who were greatly given to it were themselves for the most part possessed by the older and Christian assumptions. Indeed we may say that throughout the 'great' period of American 'liberal religion,' a strange contradiction or dichotomy marked those who were classified as 'liberal' leaders. Their explicit faith was such that it would in the end destroy the assumptions they unconsciously took for granted. The whole story is too complicated and involved for our detailed study here; it must suffice to point out that the 'liberals' were living largely on the inheritance of their fathers, without recognizing that they were squandering that inheritance. Now that the 'acids of modernity' have eaten away the residuum of their faith, we can see that 'liberal Christianity,' in the sense in which we have defined it, has its own share of responsibility for the contemporary situation. And we can understand how a point of view like that of John Dewey, in his *Common Faith*, can follow directly from the reduction of Christianity undertaken and accomplished by the 'liberals' of the period from 1880 to 1920.

It was in the year 1920 that the first signs of a resurgent 'orthodoxy' were seen. For at that time a few Americans, who followed reports and fashions in Europe, noted the appearance of Karl Barth, the Swiss theologian, on the horizon of Christian thought. The movement then inaugurated has continued to gain strength, until today in every Christian school, college, and seminary 'orthodoxy' is increasing its hold, while the 'liberalism' of the earlier period is losing ground. The story is a familiar one, far too familiar to need repeating here. First among the great in Europe and then in American seminaries, interest revived in the old theologies. It was not Karl Barth alone who did this; Emil Brunner, at first Barth's ally and later his opponent, was read here and later came to America to teach. Others were soon driven from their homes in Europe because of the Nazi movement and found refuge in the new world. For years Reinhold Niebuhr was moving 'right, theologically,' and although he disowns the name of 'neo-orthodox,' his influence in that direction has been enormous. Today few reputable theologians in the American religious world are 'liberals'; in one sense or another, with many variations in emphasis and stress, the outstanding theologians are, by their own profession, 'confessional' or 'neo-orthodox' or 'orthodox.' It is often worth one's theological reputation to defend any of the theses of 'old-fashioned liberalism' (how the leaders of that school would have shuddered at being thought 'old-fashioned'!). In fact, one of the grave dangers today, as we have previously quoted from the old German saying, is that 'the baby will be emptied out with the bath water.'

It is obvious that the 'man in the pew' has not kept pace with the 'preacher in the pulpit.' Although at recent conferences of clergy and meetings of seminarians all doubt has been killed in regard to the victory of a broadly 'orthodox' point of view, the great majority of American layfolk—those Americans, roughly numbering half the population of the land, who belong to Christian bodies and at least sometimes 'go to church' —are still in the 'liberal' era. The people are puzzled and perplexed by their ministers, for they have not been prepared to hear sermons such as are now thundered from pulpits from Maine to California. Before the war, the situation was not quite so odd; now that we have gone through the war, the clergy have become bolder and plainer in speech—perhaps because they have been enabled by these events to read 'the signs of the times' and feel that they *must* speak. But the layfolk, by and large, have not read the signs the way their pastors have read them. The war has had very little effect on the typical American attitude toward life and the great majority of our people simply cannot understand what has happened. There is in some quarters, of course, a resurgence of the old-fashioned 'fundamentalism,' which never quite died out in 'the Bible belt'; this resurgence is hardly very important in the over-all picture, which still remains predominantly one in which a 'liberal,' highly ethical interpretation of Christianity is accepted—accepted, at any rate, consciously and explicitly, despite the utterly different assumptions that, as we have seen, govern most Americans in an unconscious and, as it were, 'atmospheric' fashion.

Let us consider some of the major emphases in the 'new orthodoxy' that has swept the seminaries, is now accepted by most of the clergy who have been emancipated from their allegiance to 'liberalism,' and will more and more permeate the Christian churches as leadership falls to the young men now being trained in the divinity schools of practically every American denomination.

The first significant emphasis is in regard to the nature of man. Briefly, it is that man is a sinner, and a sinner in the most terrible sense. No longer is it sufficient to portray man as ill-informed, sadly uneducated, and requiring only information and inspiration. His situation is far worse than that. Man is depraved, whether or not 'totally depraved'; he is self-centered, proud, lustful. He is appallingly egocentric. His whole perspective is wrong and so everything he looks at is seen in a viciously false way. But it is not only that he cannot see straight. Even if he could, he is so impotent that he could not do right. His will is not merely weakened; it is perverted, so that he inevitably wills that which is bad both for him and for his fellows. Above all, when he thinks that he is acting rightly, he is guilty of the worst of all evils—for then he is proudly assuming himself to be master of his destiny and the center of the universe, whereas in fact he is absurdly and pretentiously putting his tiny self where it can never be, in the place that God alone can occupy. His vision is perverted; his desires are perverted; his will is perverted.

Nor is this true of man only as individual; it is even more true of man as social being. When sinful men get together, they are worse than when they are alone, for while individual man can be partly 'moralized,' society remains 'immoral.' The worst impulses and instincts of perverted human nature are released in social ways; you can never trust man in the mob. The whole situation is something given to us by the fact of our being human, by the fact that we are men. There is a tendency in some quarters to regard finitude itself as sinful; and although the wiser minds in our newer 'orthodoxy' protest this point, they find themselves hard put to explain their utter pessimism about man's existential condition without falling into a similar pessimism about the evil nature of created things.

The writer is by no means prepared to subscribe to this picture as being fully true. The fact remains that this violent denunciation of man and his society shows the direction in which theological writing and teaching has been moving. It need hardly be said that it is worlds apart from the optimism and perfectionism of 'liberalism,' and utterly at odds with the common assumptions of the American mind as we described them in our last chapter.

A second emphasis follows immediately; it is on the need for redemption. If man is in such a dire state, he can by no means extricate himself. He is deep in a quagmire and requires a helping hand to lift him out. So the newer stress is on the *saving* of man from his degradation. But because he is so terribly perverted, and because his social environment is likewise perverted, this redemption cannot be accomplished in a full sense—it must be 'in principle,' as one of the 'new' theologians has put it. By faith that there is a Saviour and by trust in him who can save, man can at least get a toe hold on solid ground; yet he is always slipping back into the muck and mud, always collapsing into his former state of depravity. He never has the guarantee that he is really 'saved' except as he hangs on by faith to the one who has stretched out a helping hand. The tendency, therefore, is to lay all the emphasis on 'justification,' and to put very little on 'sanctification' or steady growth in grace. It can be seen that this is a very extreme position, which has its values and its dangers. But it can be seen also that the emphasis on the need for salvation, and the rather uncertain nature of its realization, is in direct opposition to older 'liberalism' and contradicts the fondest assumptions of the American mind, with its bland confidence in man and his works, its optimism and good cheer, its assurance that things are 'getting better all the time.'

The third important 'orthodox' emphasis is on the transcendence of God. In the old 'liberal' days, this doctrine was minimized if not altogether denied—deity was an immanent force, a drive or power within nature. Today, the orientation is quite different: God is 'wholly other,' so much so that there is not only a distinction between him and his world, but an absolute and total gulf. The transcendence of God is stressed to the near exclusion of his immanence, with the result that the concept of deity often appears to approximate seventeenth and eighteenth century deism more than Christian theism. In any event, God is believed to be entirely *other than* and to a considerable degree *outside* the created world. If man is to be saved, he must be saved from beyond the world; hence the tendency, perhaps unconscious, is to exalt God in such a fashion that it is often problematical whether he can really save anything or anybody. The negative theology of the early Middle Ages has come back with a vengeance. But this emphasis is coupled with another, which moderates it somewhat—the importance, indeed the utter necessity, of revelation.

Since man cannot reach up to God, both because man is finite and because he is sinful, God must come down to man. In Jesus Christ he has done this, insists the 'new orthodoxy.' The Word of God enters human history, although Jesus as a human *model* is decidedly minimized. The centrality of Christ in this connection is remarkable; any other 'revelation' is regarded with suspicion, ranging from Barth's loyal disciples with their denial, to the acceptance by the majority of 'new' the-

ologians in America of an extremely vague 'general revelation.' All would feel that none of this is important or
significant without the fact of Christ to give it meaning and value. For many, revelation tends to cut across
rather than to crown human nature and human reason.
The 'neo-orthodox' are not likely to agree with St.
Thomas's dictum, *gratia tollit non abtulit naturam.*
Since they do not believe that man is *capax deitatis,*
they must necessarily see revelation as unrelated to
human nature and its concerns, except as humanity is
a weak instrument taken somewhat arbitrarily for use
by God. The influence of Kierkegaard has been important here; and the catastrophic view of God's action
upon man, so significant for the 'new orthodox,' seems
to reflect the distrust felt by him about any portrayal
of a 'regular' and 'settled' divine work in the world.

The newer conception of revelation is obviously at
odds with 'liberalism,' which insisted on the priority of
inspiration and tended to equate it with revelation. It
is also at odds with the common American assumption
that man can and must help himself, since that is all he
can really count on. 'If God helps us at all,' the typical
American is likely to feel, 'he helps those who help
themselves.' Dr. William Temple in his book *Nature,
Man, and God* suggested a theory of revelation that has
had some influence among the 'new orthodox,' although
it seems to many of them to be too temperate and medi-
ating. Temple's view, which insists that revelation is
'the coincidence of divinely-guided event and divinely-
guided apprehension,' is very close to (in fact is a development of) traditional Christian theology with its

trust in the limited power of the human reason; for this reason, the theologians of the 'orthodox' school are more inclined to follow thinkers like Emil Brunner, who in *Revelation and Reason* maintains that the divine disclosure cuts straight across human reason and is verified only by the testimony of the Holy Spirit. It is fair to add, however, that Brunner in his latest writings seems to be modifying his position, and in particular gives high praise to such a philosophical work as A. E. Taylor's *The Faith of a Moralist,* which is entirely in the mainstream of Christian thought.

Again, the 'new orthodoxy' is strong on the eschatological element in Christianity. The 'last things'—the fact of death, the reality of judgment, the possible destinies of heaven and hell—are once again to the fore. The eschatology has been reworked, but it is present in its fullness. We stand constantly under the mercy of God, we are told; but above all, we stand under the judgment of God. Human life reaches its finality in death, a fact that signalizes both the limitation of man as a mortal and the utter necessity for his finding his meaning, if his life is to have significance, in something other than self. The content of the ideas of heaven and hell has not been very clearly defined; yet the direction of the human soul is toward one or the other of these, depending upon whether a man has or has not been saved by grace through faith. With this eschatological stress has come a new concern for the doctrine of the resurrection of the body. There is no natural immortality of the soul, it is said; or if there is, it matters little; the Christian belief is that the body shall be raised—

and this is rightly taken in the sense that the total personality is what must be saved. The eschatological stress is the point where we begin to see the place of the symbolic in the 'new orthodoxy.' We are told that concerning absolute beginnings and absolute endings we can form no conceptual patterns; hence we must talk in pictures. Niebuhr in the latter part of his Gifford lectures, *The Nature and Destiny of Man*, discusses resurrection as the major emphasis in Christian eschatology and interprets it in a symbolical fashion.

'Liberalism' was not much interested in 'the last things,' and its view of man's destiny was more Greek than Hebrew. Man's soul was immortal, if anything could be said about it at all; certainly the notion of resurrection was thought to be crude and materialistic. As for our current American assumptions, there is no genuine eschatology here and very little lively belief in any life beyond this world; hence the newer 'orthodox' emphasis speaks once again in contradiction to our contemporary outlook. Incidentally, it is odd that even the recent war, with its long list of dead, does not seem to have altered effectively the American attitude in regard to 'the last things'; we still disregard the fact that man dies and our point of view is adequately reflected in the 'mortician's' delight in painting up and arranging a corpse so that it will bear the greatest possible resemblance to a living, though sleeping, body.

One or two points may be mentioned by way of concluding this analysis of the major emphases of the new 'orthodoxy.' The first of these is that the Church has been rediscovered. Whatever the differences in expression, theologians everywhere are writing and talking enthusiastically about the *Una Sancta*. Indeed, ecumenicity, as it is called, has tended to become something of a fad. But there can be no doubt that the movement is away from subjective and strictly personal religion toward a more objective and corporate expression of Christianity—that is to say, toward the Church of the ages and the Church of the whole *orbis terrarum*. The second is that religion is being stressed in its own right, without reduction to morality or ethics. There are certainly moral and ethical implications that follow from Christian faith; on the other hand, it is felt that religion —or better, faith in the Christian sense as response to God's saving action—stands on its own feet and is *sui generis*.

Here too we find a disagreement with 'liberalism,' which always stressed the subjective side of religion even when it was concerned to emphasize its social values and tended increasingly to assimilate religion to ethics, so that a man's faith was not so important as his behavior, while good behavior was often regarded as a satisfactory substitute for faith. Furthermore, these newer ideas are also contrary to those of the contemporary American culture, which assumes that religion is a man's subjective concern and, in any case, is significant only in so far as it inspires him to act according to standards adjudged by one criterion or another to be effective in making him a 'good citizen.'

The present writer does not share in all the ideas in the newer 'orthodoxy.' His own position (as an Anglican who stands in the broad Catholic tradition rather

than in the Protestant movement) is such that he is compelled to find certain truths and values in the older
'liberalism' as well as in much of the newer 'orthodoxy.'
In consequence, his position would undoubtedly seem
ambiguous to many from both sides. But that is beside
the point; the fact is that the theological scene in America has changed remarkably, and in the direction we
have indicated. Therefore, any particular personal position—or that of a religious communion such as the writer's, which is not in the mainstream of American Protestant life, yet is strongly influenced by it—must be held
in the face of the newer movements, as it must also be
held in the face of the actual cultural situation and the
generally accepted assumptions of the American people.

We do have the right, however, to inquire whether
the newer 'orthodoxy' is really consonant with 'the faith
of the ages.' We must consider the degree to which
newer 'orthodoxy' is indeed truly *orthodox*. By the
standard set in the traditional theologies of the Church,
especially in the great formative period of the first three
or four centuries, what can we say of it?

Briefly, we might put the answer in this fashion. The
newer point of view is closer, in most respects, to
ancient orthodoxy than was the 'liberalism' of yesterday; yet in some of its emphases, it tends to minimize
important elements in traditional orthodoxy to the
point of giving a false picture of Christianity. Let us develop this criticism in more detail by considering two of
the emphases in rediscovered 'orthodox' thought.

The first is the picture of man. It is true that orthodoxy, in the traditional sense, regarded man as a sinner. It is true that the doctrine of original sin was held. But at the same time, the ancient Fathers were very clear that since man is the creature of God, he is still in the image of God, even if that image is badly damaged by sin. Man is not utterly ruined, even though he is badly wounded. The symbol for this belief was the assertion that man was originally 'righteous,' with the capacity for free communion with God and with grace to enable him to enjoy this communion; by his own choice he lost this capacity and the grace that goes with it. Yet his reason is not totally perverted, his will is not entirely twisted, and his desires are not directed solely toward that which is evil. There is still an undergirding from God, a continuing work of grace, which holds him in being and makes him able to respond with God's help, albeit imperfectly, to those glimpses of the good that are vouchsafed him. Certainly he cannot respond in an adequate and satisfactory fashion. The doctrine of man that the Church has traditionally held may be called, indifferently, semi-Augustinianism (in which the emphasis is laid on man's radical imperfection) or semi-Pelagianism (in which the emphasis is laid on man's capacity for redemption and for the relative fulfilment of God's will for him). Here there is a balance that seems to be lacking in the newer 'orthodoxy,' while the profound insight of that theology into man's absolute dependence on, and need for, divine grace is maintained. On the other hand, the confidence in man that 'liberalism' so proudly proclaimed is corrected by a deeper understanding of the depths of man's dilemma, while its insistence that human nature is not essentially evil is given its due place in the total scheme.

Or take the doctrine of the divine transcendence, about which we have already made some observations. God is believed by the older orthodoxy to belong to a different order of being from the created world; he is indeed 'other' than man. Yet he pervades and penetrates the creation, as well as the limited being of man himself. God not only creates, but he also sustains the world; he works through it by his Word and his Spirit, so that 'in him' all things, as well as man, 'live and move and have their being.' In the phrase used by Baron von Hügel to express this traditional Christian conviction, 'the world is panentheistic'—that is, all is *in* God. When St. Athanasius describes the world as an *organon* (an instrument or vehicle) through which and in which God works, and argues for the Incarnation in Christ as a particular, concentrated, and therefore decisively saving instance of this 'organistic' operation, he speaks for the whole tradition of which he is such a distinguished representative. The ancient faith maintained both the transcendence and the immanence of God. As 'liberalism' insisted, God is indeed in his whole creation—or, as St. Thomas Aquinas put it, his whole creation is present to him at every point, and its significance is in the fact that he is so immanent. On the other hand, as the newer 'orthodoxy' insists, he is transcendent over that creation, since he is unexhausted by it and is in his own proper being utterly inexhaustible. Two lines from a medieval writer expresses this idea perfectly:

Intra cuncta nec inclusus,
extra cuncta nec exclusus.

It would be possible to go through the whole list of major emphases in our newer 'orthodoxy' and find further instances of a certain lack of proportion. It is easy to understand why this has occurred—the very necessity for contradicting the extremes of 'liberalism' made it nearly inevitable that the reaction would go too far in the opposite direction. Yet it is regrettable that this has happened, because the danger is that those who hear the newer 'orthodoxy' either will be swept off their feet by its blanket assertions, or, repelled by what seem to be serious overstatements, will not recognize the values that are really there. In fact, something of this latter sort has happened among us already—which may explain why there has been a certain reaction, not very strong but still important, on the part of non-believers in Christianity, who lambaste all orthodoxy because it represents in their judgment a libel on man and nature. We say that the reaction is not very strong, simply because there are not many non-believers who bother much about movements of Christian thought; we say that still it is important, because the attitude of non-believers is always significant to the Christian Church, whose task is to win men to the faith and not to 'put them off' in any way not utterly unavoidable.

This is not our present concern, however. We have wished simply to indicate that while it is correct to speak, as we have done, of the 'recovery of orthodoxy' in the non-Roman religious world in America, and the

strengthening that thereby has been given the more traditional theology in a communion such as the Anglican
or Episcopal Church, this does not necessarily mean that
the position of the 'new orthodox' school is at every
point identical with that held historically by the mainstream of Christian thought. It is of course inevitable
that new situations will produce new emphases and a
new understanding of old ones. On the whole, we may
confidently assert that the swing to the right has been
salutary for Christianity, since it has carried with it an
interest in and a serious concern for the traditional
theologies of the Christian Church. This is welcome because in the past fifty years the average American theologian, outside the Catholic communions and sometimes inside them, was so intent upon 'adjusting Christianity' to what was called 'modern thought' that he
often forgot what exactly he was called to do; instead
of seeking ways in which perennial Christian truths
could be tellingly presented in modern language, he
frequently rejected those truths and offered 'another
gospel' instead of the Christian gospel. On the other
hand, it is not at all impossible that in the very violence
of reaction from this 'reductionist' kind of thought, we
shall witness a growth of sheer intransigeance, with no
concern whatever for necessary 're-statement.' Such was
never the way of the great theologians of the past; start-
ing with St. Paul, it has been their concern to interpret
the faith in such a fashion that men in their age could
accept it, while they have always conceded that new
truth does in fact become known as the centuries pass—
new truth that both deepens man's understanding of

the faith and also must find its right place in the total perspective of that faith.

We shall try to indicate, in our concluding chapter, the need for what we venture to call 'dynamic orthodoxy,' using these words to mean a faith that holds firmly to the traditional position of the Christian Church on all essentials, and at the same time is alert to new truth, wherever that may be found. It is possible that such a dynamic orthodoxy may conserve whatever values were present in the old 'liberalism,' while it is also clear in regard to the truth of the emphases in the recovered 'orthodoxy' of our time. One can only hope that this is the case—a hope that is a strong and firm expectation, rather than a feeble wishful thought.

To return to an earlier point, we wish to lay the greatest possible stress upon the gulf that exists at the present moment between the clergy and the laity, so far as rediscovered 'orthodoxy' is concerned. The gulf was not so wide when the clergy were content with the old 'liberal' conception of Christianity, for in that case they were only enunciating what was the religious outlook of their people, even if they went beyond them in seeing deeper and broader implications—as, for example, in the clergy's insistence that the social gospel, as it was called, was necessarily involved in the Christian 'way of life.' But now that the minister has lost the old cheerful confidence in man, questions the supreme value of education as the means of human salvation, and insists on the absolute priority of God over all human interests and endeavors, the laity are puzzled and are likely to complain that religion no longer is presented as having contact with the real world of their experience. There is something in this complaint, as we shall see; yet the situation does confront the Christian Church with a serious problem, which it must some-how sólve if it can hope to have a word that speaks to our present condition. This was indicated by the lay-man who remarked that he wanted sermons that would help him in his daily life, but all he got nowadays was talk about man's depravity and helplessness. He may have been wrong-headed and misguided, but he was not without sǫme justification in his complaint.

In any event, there is no doubt about the rediscovery of 'orthodoxy' in the American theological world and its almost vociferous reassertion in the pulpits of Ameri-can churches. Nor is there any doubt that among those who for any reason whatever are interested in religious matters, there is a new respect for theology. It was next to impossible for secular thinkers to have any respect for much of the older 'liberalism'; as someone re-marked, the conception of God that such a theology maintained was one that 'no self-respecting man could entertain.' Nowadays, it seems to be felt that Christian-ity at least has a position and can be respected for main-taining it, even when its beliefs are thought to be in-credible and its major assumptions impossible for our contemporary world.

This point brings us to the concluding consideration of the present chapter. The newer 'orthodoxy' has ap-proached the whole question of religious faith from the side of man's dilemma rather than from an attempt to make place for religion in a total world view in which science is dominant. The obstacle to faith is no longer the supposed contradiction between evolution and creation, between a scientific world and the religious sentiment, et cetera, such as agitated the minds of many of us when we were young. The real obstacle now is what might roughly be called a cultural one—that is, it is the problem of relating a vigorous religious faith to a cultural situation in which man's problems seem not only to be insoluble by concerted human effort, but to be indeed insoluble altogether.

The cynicism of the 'intellectuals' of our day seems to be close to the position of the 'new orthodoxy,' for both begin with a thorough pessimism about man. For the majority of Americans, however, we may confidently assert that a fundamentally bourgeois point of view is all they have to live by. That point of view is summed up in the assumptions we have described. If one who holds it happens also to be a religious person, he interprets religion either consciously or unconsciously in this vein, or he is the victim of schizophrenia. If he is not religious, he 'gets along' by the simple expedient of living only superficially and by contenting himself with the immediacies of existence.

It is to this situation, then, that the rediscovered 'orthodoxy' of our day must address itself. In the next chapter, we shall seek to consider some of the values and some of the dangers of that 'new orthodoxy,' as it is brought into contact with the life of the American people, always remembering that it is impossible to do more than suggest and intimate. One thing we must never forget, although it is something that those of us who are theologically-minded are all too likely to forget. That is the truth that men are almost infinitely different in outlook and attitude; hence, what is dangerous for one may be invaluable for another, while what is helpful to one may come close to making life meaningless to another. We cannot give an easy and complete answer to any human problem, or meet the needs of any given social scene 'without remainder'; this kind of humility is required in any and every attempt to appraise the relationship of Christianity, whatever its forms, to the actual concrete situation in which men find themselves. Even the best of theologians, even the wisest of observers of the contemporary scene, must remember that to God alone may be ascribed that omniscience to which 'all hearts are open, all desires known,' and from which 'no secrets are hid.'

4] *Values and Dangers in the* *'Orthodox' Reaction*

Baron Friedrich von Hügel, to whose profound thinking so many of us are deeply indebted, always said everything he could in praise of a book he was reviewing before he went on to indicate the errors or inadequacies in the volume. It was natural to his generous and catholic mind to do this; and we may well follow his example in our consideration, not of a book, but of a movement. First we shall notice some of the values that may be discovered in the return to 'orthodoxy' among Christian thinkers. After we have discussed these positive qualities, we shall be better prepared to point out some of the dangers that may lurk in that movement. In this chapter, our interest is not with theological matters directly, but with the way the 'new orthodoxy' bears upon the American scene and makes a happy or unhappy contribution to the changed cultural situation in which we find ourselves today.

If there is any one thing the American mind needs today, it is a challenge that will force it to give attention to the utter inadequacy, not to say fallacy, of the common assumptions by which we live. 'Liberalism' was unable to do this, because 'liberalism' was in many ways a reflection of the native American mind, attitude, and character. The 'liberal' theology, when there was one, was often a kind of intellectual sanction for the 'way of life' to which Americans were devoted; when there was no theology, but simply an interest in 'religion' as a 'good thing,' the result all too often was that the typical American felt that Christianity's principal importance was that it provided a certain dynamic for those qualities of good citizenship that commended themselves to all right-thinking people. It is not necessary to have attended many patriotic rallies to have learned that the 'use' of religion was the point always stressed, if it were found necessary to bring such matters into an oration. The conclusion of addresses by senators and congressmen, not to mention higher governmental dignitaries, usually includes a brief reference to religion, in which the old 'liberal' ideas are expressed—and naturally so, for these liberal ideas give precisely the kind of 'holy aura' needed to save the addresses from being sheer nationalism, chauvinism, appeals for power, or sops to the public mind.

The 'orthodoxy' that has been revived in our day is very different from this. It takes a definite and clear position, with assertions that cut directly across many of our American assumptions. For instance, it is plain that the bold and frank proclamation of God as the utterly sovereign transcendent Lord is hardly a sanction for a naive identification of deity with America's 'manifest destiny,' an identification that, however disguised, has become all too popular these days. When we consider a better side of our American life—namely, the deep interest of humanitarians and reformers in the improvement of social, economic, and industrial life—we find that the 'neo-orthodoxy' of a Reinhold Niebuhr has no place for the sentimentalism and perfectionism that so many of our reformers exhibit.

Furthermore, 'orthodoxy' is an established and, so to say, integrated view of God and the world; it can therefore speak with a wholeness and totality that offer opposition to the usual American dismissal of religion as an adjectival and peripheral concern, acceptance of which depends on the taste and fancy of the believer. All men are lost, says 'orthodoxy'; this means that all men, quite without regard for their particular tastes or fancies, need to be saved by God. It is a long time since we have had any such position to oppose the typical American mind, for even the fundamentalists did not take quite that stand; they managed to accommodate themselves, on the whole, to some of the worst features of American life. Roman Catholicism has offered a total outlook, but in America, even yet, Roman Catholicism is not the dominant religion, and our culture, as the Romanists themselves are now recognizing, has been largely, if not entirely, a Protestant culture, both in origin and in general development. 'Liberalism' offered an outlook scarcely different from that of the secular world. Hence we are confronting a novel situation, which has by no means developed fully, but one that is likely to provide an interesting spectacle in the next few decades.

A recent volume by Dr. Niebuhr, entitled *Children of Light and Children of Darkness,* is significant for another value in the rediscovery of 'orthodoxy.' In this book, the writer seeks to prove that democracy has been poorly served by those who sought to defend it during the past fifty years; the defense, he shows, was on the basis of a completely mistaken 'liberalistic estimate' both of man and of his world, and was rooted in a false philosophy. Hence he argues that if democracy is to have any intellectual justification against other possible orderings of society, it must be defended in terms of a realistic appraisal of man and his world. Dr. Eduard Heimann, in his *Freedom and Order,* has maintained that a basic philosophy, with a religious orientation, is essential if democracy is to be defended with any genuine validity today. Now both of these men are in the company of the 'neo-orthodox,' whether or not they accept the name. Both are in reaction from the vagueness of nineteenth and early twentieth century 'liberalism.' Both are seriously concerned to deny the common assumptions of American life and to put in their place a more Christian understanding of man and his destiny. It is exactly here, then, that the 'new orthodoxy' has a particular value. For on every hand, among thinking people, the confidence in the validity and even in the value of the democratic way is being questioned; although we were told that the recent war was fought, like the last one, for the defense of democracy, we are not so sure that this was the case nor are we so certain that democracy, as it has been presented in some quarters, is worth saving. Yet most of us would admit that the line taken by democracy has been better for mankind than that taken by dictatorships or sheer authoritarian regimes. This is quite apart from what may be the likely future for our American society. Our point is that if 'orthodoxy' can provide, as Niebuhr and Heimann, among others, think it can, a defense of democracy that takes account of the facts about human nature and social groups, it will have a unique value for our contemporary American scene and will influence enormously the culture of our time.

When 'orthodoxy' gains a hold upon the believer, it can do something for him that is not often enough recognized. We have seen that there is a kind of unconscious schizophrenia in the average devout believer these days. But when a Christian comes to see the definite position of the Christian Church, this hidden split can become, so to say, overt. We are not speaking here in terms appropriate to psychiatry; we are simply using convenient words to indicate a real situation. The tensions and strains, resulting from the attempt to live two quite different existences in one's inner self, can now become open and aboveboard. When this happens, these tensions and strains have a certain healthy and fruitful quality, for the believer is no longer under any illusions about his dual citizenship, and is seeking consciously to make such reconciliations and accommodations in immediate respects as shall guarantee and guard his primary allegiance to the Christian faith and standards in an ultimate respect. Kierkegaard puts this point

very well. It will be recalled that in his wonderful
parable of Abraham and Isaac, he comes to the point
where he says that our duty is to live 'relatively in regard to the relative, and absolutely in regard to the absolute.' He means that in the realm of worldly activities,
it is necessary to make such accommodations as shall
render human life possible, while all the time there is
that final and all-inclusive allegiance to the will of God
that saves one's particular accommodations from being
mere expediency or 'relativity,' in our ordinary American sense of the latter word. To bring this out in the
open, and to face it plainly and without equivocation,
is a healthy and fruitful thing; to live in tension of this
kind, accepted and recognized, is also healthy and fruitful. For it means merely facing the facts of our dual
citizenship and our divided loyalty; and, after facing
the facts, putting primary things in the first place and
secondary things in the second place, while we recognize that all that we do involves both 'absolute' and
'relative.' Then we can honestly and rightly make judg-
ments and choose among 'goods,' knowing what we do
and why we do it.

In so far as 'orthodoxy' can do this for the American
Christian, it will have made an enormous contribution
to his religious, and even to his emotional, health. For
the very fact of the unconscious character of our 'split'
is its great danger for both religious and emotional
wholeness.

American culture, at least in recent years, has not
been noted for any great profundity; it has been pretty
much on the surface, lacking what we have called 'the

dimension of depth.' 'Orthodoxy' can do a service here that will be immeasurable. It can force Americans, even if only in reaction from its claims, to consider more seriously and deeply the nature of man and his destiny. It can in this way help to 'show up' the superficiality of our American assumptions about the meaning of experience. If we read the treatment of human nature in such a book as John Dewey's early study *Human Nature and Experience,* we are struck by the triviality of his portrayal. Our educational leaders in teachers' colleges and elsewhere likewise have a simple and somewhat superficial picture of human nature. Our novelists tend to write about 'what happens,' rather than about the depths of man's being. When Henry James probed deeply into human psychology, motivation, and desire, he was regarded by many as intentionally recondite and obscure. Foreigners visiting the United States are struck by this superficiality; they usually attribute it to the fact that we are a 'new country,' but we can hardly claim that excuse—indeed, one could say that in colonial and early republican days, American culture was quite as deep and profound as European. It is only since the acceptance of a pragmatic view of life, and under the wide influence of 'liberal' religious ideas, that the harm has been done. It can be said confidently that the common American assumptions are both responsible for and a reflection of the superficiality of a culture more concerned with actions than with character, with gadgets than with men, and with results than with reasons.

Conversely, 'orthodoxy' holds a view of man that penetrates to the hidden depths of his being, that recognizes that *is-ness* is the most important fact about human nature, and that insists on the need for a radical reorientation of human nature as the condition for human salvation. It sees the mystery in man, and behind that mystery it sees the mystery of the universe and the mystery of the God who creates it. Never content with surface appearance, it looks long enough at things to understand that their meaning is to be known only by introspection and intuitive apprehension, rather than by external observation or reports on pointer readings. Experience during the past few years has led some thinkers to see more deeply and ponder more carefully the 'sense' of things. 'Orthodoxy' can strengthen this tendency; and in circles where its influence has reached, it has already produced a discontent with the glibness of educational psychology and instrumental philosophy and an insistence that there is more in man than the 'social sciences' can discern.

These, then, are some of the values we may find in the 'orthodox' movement. Our list is by no means exhaustive; it is, as we have said before, intended only to be suggestive. It will be the same with our discussion of the other side of the picture—the dangers that may be found in the 'new orthodoxy.' That there are dangers may not be too obvious; in our enthusiasm for this welcome return to a more traditional view of Christianity, we may overlook the fact that while it offers salutary correction to many of our contemporary American assumptions and could do much for the deepening and strengthening of our culture, at the same time it has dangers that are likely to have disastrous consequences.

The first of the dangers in the 'new orthodoxy' is its lack of a point of contact with the American scene. The particular emphases strong in this revival are so utterly contradictory to the older 'liberalism' and so completely opposed to the common American assumptions, that they seem to come from another world so far as the average American is concerned. It may very well be inevitable that this should be so; after all, if the position of 'orthodoxy' as it is now understood, cuts across the whole cultural situation in America, it cannot be helped. But the fact remains that it does negate the 'values' and the 'loyalties' to which Americans now give themselves.

The remark of Dr. Tillich in regard to the way Karl Barth lost the chance of winning the loyalty of young Germany would seem to be to the point here. If the 'new orthodoxy' is to be in *absolute* opposition to everything American, if it is to cut across *all* assumptions and deny *all* loyalties that appeal to the typical citizen, it may end by doing more harm than good. For it can cut the ground from under the older 'liberalism,' without vitiating the common assumptions that were at least somewhat ameliorated by the 'liberal' influence. The result will be sheer secularism, without even a tinge of religious spirit on the part of those who are not won over to 'orthodoxy.' There may be a real value in some of the assumptions governing American life; some of them may not be viciously unchristian but may be a perverted expression of certain historically Christian ideas. If the 'new orthodoxy' were willing to make terms with these ideas, or with a few of them, it might 'ransom the times.' In any case, it would offer some point of contact with the times.

To use a simple illustration, we should indicate that while the appeal to this-worldly standards and goals is plainly unchristian, yet there is value in this world and its affairs. Christianity is deeply concerned for the improvement of human society, the realization of personality, and those other 'goods' that appeal to the ordinary American, such as living the best kind of life he can in the here-and-now. We ought to show that Christianity is not a 'pie-in-the-sky' religion; its other-worldliness is not opposed to a genuine interest in this world and its affairs; its interest is not to force men to deny their natural inclinations and desires, but to order them toward their best good: the full realization of all their possibilities, here *and* hereafter. Too often, despite leaders like Niebuhr, the preaching of 'orthodoxy' has meant that secular interests are still regarded on a purely this-worldly basis, even if socialism rather than capitalism is advocated. The incarnational and sacramental point of view, which would guarantee the religious value of this world and its organizations and interests, is not taught because God is so utterly transcendent and man so utterly sinful that there can be little relation between them, save as helpless sinner on the one hand and intervening Saviour on the other. Faced with a religion primarily 'salvation-centered,' America may turn away from all orthodoxy to that kind of religiosity already popular in our midst—an American version of the 'German Christian' movement, which simply sanctions and canonizes American ideals and the

American 'way of life.' It is a danger against which we must ever be on guard.

Another danger, actual or potential, is that 'orthodoxy' will bring with it a hopeless and perhaps even a cynical attitude toward the problems we face today. We have seen this in some of the younger men in theological circles today. If anything and everything men do is sinful, then it seems useless to do anything at all. It has been pointed out that interest in social action, for example, is markedly less real among the followers of Niebuhr than among the followers of the old 'liberals' like Harry F. Ward. Niebuhr himself is a radical in politics—although in recent years he seems to have become somewhat more conservative in opinion; yet the hundreds of clergy who have come under his spell have not always been filled with his radical spirit. Many of them have kept to the 'left,' of course; but many more, if our observations are at all sound, have accepted the 'Niebuhrian' position as a *religious* point of view that has indicated that perfectionism is wrong and hence has suggested that since man is now a sinner and always will be one, he can do very little to change the situation his sin produces.

Furthermore, the constant attack of some of the 'orthodox' on human reason has tended to present the sorry spectacle of a group of men who use their reason to deny their reason. They believe that nothing men discover is really true; they say that suspicion is the proper attitude that ought to be taken in regard to all human activities, intellectual or otherwise. A subtle distrust of natural human goodness is likewise common—

indeed, we might say that *anything* attributed to man is questioned from the start. There is obviously considerable truth in this belief; yet it cuts the nerve of all human action, tends to regard all human affection as well as all human thinking as not merely imperfect but continuously perverse, and in the end it may lead to a cynicism and despair bearing very little resemblance to the attitude characteristic of Christianity through the centuries. Historically, Christian thinkers have had no doubt about the limitations of human nature, nor have they hesitated to speak strongly of the sinfulness that vitiates it. But they have not taken toward it such a jaundiced attitude as that of some of the theologians of our own day.

It is difficult to see how the 'new orthodoxy' is going to make very much sense to our age if it is content simply to rest in its loud denunciations. It is precisely here, once more, that we find another danger in the revival. Cynicism in regard to human nature is certainly a danger; utter despair is another, coupled, as it may be, with the feeling that no matter what one may attempt, it is sure to come out badly in the end. A third danger is a carping and hypercritical mood. It is quite easy to see the way in which a clear-sighted thinker can discern error and imperfection in any and every proposal made for the amelioration of our contemporary situation; furthermore, it does not require much more than common sense to recognize that men support almost any program from a variety of motives. But the critical spirit that is an invaluable component of any sound intellect can be carried to such an extreme that time is spent on nothing but destructive and negative criticism, much of it merely captious. It was once remarked that a leading weekly in this country was 'constitutionally unable to see any good in anything.' Perhaps a danger of the 'new orthodox' is that they too may become 'constitutionally unable to see any good in anything.' It is hardly an exaggeration that in so far as this is true, these thinkers are taking a position not consonant with the point of view represented by the great thinkers of the Christian tradition. In any case, a carping and captious attitude toward all human enterprise is bound to have unhappy repercussions.

Furthermore, even if it be true, and unquestionably it is true, that human reason is profoundly limited and that man's conclusions must always be watched lest they be spoiled by 'special pleading' and 'wishful thinking,' it is also true that the human reason is the only instrument we have for discovering a whole area of truth and the only instrument that may be sufficiently checked so that the margin of error can be restricted. Even when we have admitted the imperfection and perversion of the human will, it is still true that the will accomplishes all done by men in this world; even if our desires are all too frequently directed toward that which is bad for us and for our human brethren, we do desire and can desire only that which *seems* good to us, however limited and fallible our judgment may be. In fact, human nature with its worst tendencies and most reprehensible drives is still not without *some* good—it can discover truth, if only occasionally; it can will the right, if only now and again; it can love the good, if only infrequently. This admission does not mean that 'liberalism' was right in its extravagant claims for man, nor does it suggest that the American assumptions about human nature are correct. But it does imply that the extreme denials and negations that sometimes come from the pens of the' newer theologians are badly in need of qualification.

Once, after a long and pessimistic lecture on the nature of man, one of the auditors is reported to have said, 'If that is true, then the only thing to do is jump in the river.' Somehow we had a sneaking sympathy for the reaction, not because we took a bright and rosy view of human nature, but because we believed that if the first account of man must be that he is a sinner, the Christian reconsideration of that account must lead to the conviction that even if he *is* a sinner he still has possibilities for good. Historical theology, as we have indicated above, began with man as 'originally righteous'; he must be restored from his 'fallen' state, it affirmed, so that he may once again be a healthy and whole creature.

It is here, in its insistence on man's near 'total depravity,' that the 'new orthodoxy' seems chiefly to have gone astray. Its almost hopeless view of man, apart from catastrophic reorientation from without, has led it to paint too dark a picture. That man needs salvation, and that it must come from outside himself, we shall readily admit. Yet we cannot limit that salvation to the specific Christian revelation, remembering, as we must, the attitude of the great historic theologies, which have always spoken of the 'uncovenanted mercies of God,' the 'work of the unincarnate Logos,' and the 'diffused effects of grace,' quite apart from the Christian gospel. The danger is that the excessively narrow view of salvation taken by many of the 'orthodox,' coupled with the extreme pessimism of their estimate of human nature, will alienate those who are ready to be convinced of the Christian faith. To the average man, this view may seem to make hash of his life and experience, when he is trying most deeply to appraise his seeking for truth and his endeavor to do right. It is not only incredible but a blasphemy upon the things that, at his best, he reverences and cherishes.

The writer hopes that he will not be mistaken here. It is not his intention to speak as a defender of the 'Pollyanna' conception of human nature; yet he cannot help feeling that a presentation of Christianity that has gone so far to the other side is hardly very close to the Christian gospel and is hardly calculated to make any appeal to those who are not peculiarly conditioned for such a message.

We must not judge the truth or the falsity of a position by its popular appeal; yet it is certainly true that Christianity has, historically, not only criticized man for his pretensions, but also crowned his goodness, wherever it might be found, as being a gift of God and worthy of commendation. This has been the condition of Christianity's growth in all parts of the world. From the day when the values of Greek culture were appreciated and incorporated into the Christian tradition, to the present moment when some have been bold enough to believe that the scientific outlook, although partial, is in its very partiality a divine gift, Christianity has appealed to men as both vindicating whatever partial truth they already knew and correcting that partial truth by setting it in a wider perspective. The 'new orthodoxy' does not seem willing to do this. It distrusts man and so it distrusts all his achievements; it tends to disregard that wider range of life which older thought ascribed to the unincarnate Word 'by whom all things were made.' Here is a serious departure from traditional Christian orthodoxy; here also is a danger that must be guarded against by those who wish to restore the sound and authentic Christian note to this or any other culture.

These dangers—and others that follow by implication —are related to the failure of the 'new orthodoxy' to make enough of what has been well described as the 'horizontal' movement of God in His world. Its attention has been given almost entirely to the 'vertical' movement, the divine down-trust. What this has meant (apart from its theological consequences in a minimizing of sanctification, of grace as power, of the necessity of sacraments, of the divine nature of the Church as the Body of Christ in a social extension, of the essential though 'fallen' goodness of the natural order, of the wide spread of revelation in many forms and in sometimes surprising places) has been that 'orthodoxy' has seemed to contradict all of the secular goods that have painstakingly been won by the race. As for the 'intellectual,' he then rejects the entire Christian tradition. He is, of course, unaware of the wider teaching and the more generous theology of an earlier day, because he has been so completely uneducated in religion. And his last state, we might say, is worse than the first. He cannot accept 'liberalism,' because its very foundations are undermined by his insight into the real facts; he will not accept the 'new orthodoxy' because he feels that it says 'No' to all he values; he has never heard of the more dynamic orthodoxy, more profound than 'liberalism' and less intransigeant than 'neo-orthodoxy.'

As for the non-intellectual, it is likely that *he* will prefer to remain in a vague 'liberalism' because 'orthodoxy' seems so intolerably severe on what he most values. Or, if he does not have any formed religion at all, he will remain content in his secular and humanistic world view because he will think that it at least makes sense of the life he actually knows and experiences, in a way that, in his judgment, the 'orthodox' revival does not. Here is tragedy, because it is this secular and humanistic world view, which is so lamentably inadequate, that has taught the erroneous notions of man and his destiny that fail us on every hand, and in a short time will actually be collapsing around us.

Hence one is compelled to say that the rediscovery of 'orthodoxy' in our day has been both a blessing and a curse. This may seem a strange remark from one who is a traditional Christian; yet it must be made. If the 'orthodox' revival could have been tempered by a more hospitable attitude toward natural truth and goodness, correcting the errors of secular humanism on the one hand and supplementing the inadequacies of 'liberalism' on the other, it would have been entirely a blessing. The intolerant and extreme overemphases of the 'newer orthodoxy,' however, have sometimes made it a curse—although that is too strong a word, and we should simply say 'a mixed blessing.' Nevertheless, in several instances it has been very close to a curse. The writer recalls a young man who reacted so violently from 'liberalism' that he became an almost complete cynic about human nature and human society, while he was at the same time a devoted and convinced believer in 'orthodox' Christianity. In another instance, a young woman who, far from being converted to Christianity when the 'new orthodoxy' was presented to her, was pushed even more deeply into a convinced secularism, because (as she honestly stated) she was utterly unable to take such a 'low' view of herself and her fellowmen.

It is perfectly clear that the whole tenor of our society is changing; the movement from an individualistic and, on the whole, laissez-faire ordering of life has proceeded so far that it cannot be stopped; the conclusion of the matter is not entirely plain, but that we are facing a change toward a new ordering of society, on corporate and co-operative lines, is sure enough. Whether this will be a democratic version of totalitarianism, a military or industrial dictatorship, a 'planned society' in which personal claims will still have their proper place and the rights of man still be safeguarded, we cannot say with any confidence. But it is in such a society, rather than in the older and familiar one, that we shall be living the day after tomorrow; it is in such a society that the Christian religion must find its place. The newer 'orthodoxy' will be both valuable and dangerous in that kind of socialized pattern.

In so far as the 'new orthodoxy' is critical of all human pretensions and achievements, holding a transcendent God to be judge of all the activities of sinful man, it will be a salutary corrective. It will insist that even the most perfect ordering of human affairs, on a secular basis, cannot give men peace and lasting happiness—man needs what Christianity calls salvation. On the other hand, in so far as the 'new orthodoxy' rejects this movement as irrelevant to faith and tends to think there is very little choice between a 'rugged individualism' and a 'planned society' since man is a sinner under any and every social structure, it will be dangerous indeed. For it will suggest to some that *laissez-faire* is the best policy, and so it will deprive the new society of the help of those who could most effectively work toward its best possible development; to others, it will suggest that because man's state is so consistently sinful, as it were, it is entirely congruous with Christian faith to remain or try to remain in the *status quo*.

Once again, it is not without reason that we remark upon the need for a criticism of the 'orthodox' attack upon 'liberalism,' a criticism that will accept the main theses but modify their statement and seek to relate them more generously to the humanitarian and 'perfectionist' spirit of American life—a spirit having its roots not only in the writings of older secular thinkers, but also in the generalizations of Christian principle that in the past have played their role in our national life and are not even yet entirely obliterated in those who are moved by compassion or indignation to seek to improve the lot of their fellowmen.

When we have seen more of the likely pattern of things to come, we shall be ready to speak of the place and function of the Christian Church in the new order. But we cannot conclude this chapter, which brings to an end our discussion of the swing back to a more traditional understanding of the Christian religion, without reaffirming our conviction that in the dialectical movement of history, much good was in fact accomplished by the older 'liberalism' and much good will be accomplished by the newer 'orthodoxy,' while each one had and has its peculiar and distinctive dangers. Perhaps it is possible, when we realize this strange dialectic, to see that what might roughly be called post-Reformation Protestant theology has been given a remarkable opportunity to work through, experimentally as it were, a variety of possible points of view; it has emerged from this movement with the possibility of approximating the balance and proportion of the pre-Reformation theology—by which we mean, of course, not the Roman Catholic position, but the traditional Catholic position classically expressed in the age of the Fathers and not too unworthily stated in what von Hügel called 'the golden Middle Ages,' the time of St. Thomas Aquinas, St. Bonaventura, and Duns Scotus.

If the writer may once again speak personally, he would remark that for him one of the unique contributions Anglicanism seems to be able to make to the religious scene is in its continuation of that great tradition, without the extremes of either 'liberalism' or the newer 'orthodoxy.' In the great Caroline divines, for example, there is a straight development from the classical theology but with due recognition of what might well be called 'the Reformation insights.' Because official Rome has lacked these insights, she has failed to enter into a large element of what used to be termed 'gospel truth,' and her utter intransigeance *vis-à-vis* Protestantism has made it impossible for her to bring her own enormous and balancing contribution to theological development in such a country as America. The writer knows of no presentation of Christianity so likely to serve the needs of our own time and place, and so loyally and centrally orthodox in the best traditional sense, as the over-all teaching of a man like Baron von Hügel, from the Roman and Catholic tradition; or the late Professor A. E. Taylor, from the Anglican and Catholic tradition; or, on the American continent and as a Protestant, Professor Paul Tillich. The last of these thinkers, although his terminology is often obscure and difficult, has so tempered his rediscovery of 'orthodoxy' by a generous recognition of the truth in 'liberalism,' and has so combined this with a profound understanding of the historical theology of the Christian Church in all its aspects, that he represents in the American Protestant scene the same wisdom and depth one finds in von Hügel and Taylor.

5] *The Emergence of a New Society*

'The world of tomorrow. . .' Newspaper advertisements and articles in periodicals have for a long time
been devoted to portraying what that world will be,
usually in terms of a vast increase in the number of
mechanical appliances, household conveniences, and
laborsaving devices. Essays and books are written telling
us about the structure of society, about education as it
will be in the new age, about the kind of religion suit-
able for it, about almost everything else that might be
suggested. On the whole, up until very recently, the
picture of the future was fairly cheerful. Now, with the
atomic bomb and the 'improvements' in 'medical warfare' (as the strange phrase has it!), the forecast is not
quite so bright. It is indeed a question whether there
will be any new world. Perhaps tomorrow there will be
only a few men and women struggling for livelihood
here and there in remote and inaccessible spots on a
devastated planet. Nor is this merely a bare possibility;
it is almost a probability, unless something is done—and
soon—to establish understanding and peaceful relations
among the nations of the earth.

But granted that the world does go on, what about the pattern of the new society? More particularly, what about the pattern of things here in America? For it is to the American scene that we are devoting our attention in this book, although we are well aware of the fact that what happens elsewhere affects us here at home just as our own social evolution has its bearing upon the affairs of men in the far corners of the globe. That America is in a process of transition is apparent to all who have eyes to see and ears to hear. What will the conclusion of that process be?

It is possible only to hint and suggest; he would be a fool who endeavored to draw a 'chart correct' of the future America, when so much seems uncertain and so little seems plain. Yet there are broad outlines that may be discerned, general lines of development that may be noted, highly probable aspects of the new society that may be charted. It is to these that we shall devote our attention.

The kind of individualism that has marked so much of our American history appears to be at an end. This does not necessarily mean that the individual counts for less or should count for less. Rather, it means that his place and the fashion in which he plays his part in society will be profoundly modified in the near future, even as it has already undergone serious change. When certain large national organizations speak of 'free enterprise' and 'the right of the individual,' they are either disingenuous or they are 'fooling themselves.' There was a time when the individual citizen in America had a fairly wide future before him; under a few restrictions, he could pretty well express himself, make his fortune, and do what he pleased, with little or no interference. The restrictions were those of common decency and public opinion, and they were rather flexible; freedom, in what now seems an extreme sense, was granted. Indeed, if one had certain privileges, he could often do exactly what he wanted, when he wanted, and as he wanted. This hardly applied to the huge number of citizens who were frequently oppressed by poverty and harassed by lack of opportunity. But it was the theory, and to some extent the fact, that 'every American could be President of the United States'—a symbolic way of saying that every individual had both the right and the capacity to 'get ahead.'

This theory is what ought to be implied in the term 'free enterprise.' Unfortunately, the term today does not mean what it says, any more than does the phrase 'rights of the individual.' That the meaning has changed as it has, is a token of the truth that old-fashioned American individualism is dead. For what these terms usually mean today is that American business, more particularly 'big business,' ought to have the right and the freedom to 'get ahead' without government interference, legal restriction, and the constant necessity of accommodating itself to the demands of labor, the requirements of public policy, and the affirmations of an awakened social conscience. That is very different from the older idea.

At every point, the individual is 'cabined, cribbed, confined.' This may be for good or for bad—that is not our interest here. The point is that from police regulations about driving speed to the Security Exchange Commission's control of the stock market, there is constant interference with the individual's self-expression. And the area of that interference is growing rapidly, so that almost no part of a citizen's life is without some measure of control.

Now it is this fact that points the way to the nature of the new society. Whatever else may be said of this coming order, it will be one of increasing control of the individual. Control will doubtless be exercised by agencies whose purpose will be regulation in the interests of what is conceived to be the common good. Some may not like this trend, others may approve it. But whether we like it or not, it is on the way and we can do little or nothing to arrest it. The best we can do is to try to direct it to a growth as sound and healthy as possible.

To the writer, this trend of American life seems right and proper. When reactionary legislation—in the sense of an attempt to react against a new thing by returning to an old one it has replaced—is employed to stop this trend, the likelihood is that the rebound will be greater than if normal development had been allowed to take place. Furthermore, he would gladly add that he feels the Christian Church has its duty in pressing for this development, in the degree that it promises to bring to more men an opportunity to live in greater happiness and security than was possible under the older regime. At the same time, he would not be unaware of the dangers—dangers that may be summed up in the simple statement that the more men are controlled, even in their own interest, the more they are in peril of losing their personal initiative and their personal integrity, and the more likely they are to become mere pawns.

The writer's views about the desirability of the change in our social pattern are of slight importance, however; what is important is the fact of the change. It is extraordinary that many who clearly discern the situation in which American society finds itself are unwilling or unable to recognize it for what it is. They permit their natural predilections to determine their vision, and frequently drum up excuses for their unwillingness to see what is actually happening. This attitude is a factor in the seriousness of the change, for the danger of rear-guard warfare is that it will confound the situation in such a way that nobody can tell what side he is fighting on. But forward-looking minds know well enough 'what the score is,' and they are bending every effort to work for such a planning of society as shall guarantee that the real goods of our older individualism shall be carried into the newer order. If we are to live in a controlled society, we may as well honestly face it and see what it implies. Only in this way can we be prepared to find ways in which genuine freedom and personal integrity can be preserved. It is not necessary that America should develop, as it appears in some respects already to be developing, into a 'police state.' The way to avoid that chance is to work for such democratic controls and such means of asserting personal rights as shall make the new society, with all its planning, one that promises the most good to the most people, with no special privileges to any particular group or class. Above all, if the Church is to 'pull its weight,' or to have a significant part in the new society, it must recognize the facts for what they are and construct its strategy in the light of them.

Here, then, we are accepting the facts and recognizing that the degree of control that will prevail in the new society will be enormously greater than that at the present moment. Our particular interest, of course, is not economic; yet we must say a word or two on this aspect of the picture. Despite the attempts to put a stop to the growing governmental management of industry —a management effected by various executive agencies, supervisory commissions, legislative enactments—it would appear that our economic life is going to be guided and regimented more and more by the over-all policies established in Washington. The recent world war marked a tremendous advance in this process; after all, it was impossible to trust to private planning and individual production schemes when so much was at stake. The consequence of this national program of production was that American industry came to feel both governmental pressure and governmental control. While these have been relaxed to a considerable extent in the postwar period, the results of the relaxation have not been very satisfactory. Discontent is so widely felt that it is likely that within a few years, granted the continued power of public opinion, there will be a return to a greater measure of economic control. Even now, with the relaxing we have mentioned, there is still sufficient control to bring yells of annoyance and cries of 'socialism' from those who believe that business and industry should be 'entirely free.'

In social welfare the amount of governmental interest and control is vastly increasing. When a conservative Republican leader like Robert A. Taft was responsible for an extension of housing under governmental agencies, we saw a sign of the times that could hardly be misread. Social security is an accepted plank in the platforms of all political groups. Unemployment and old-age insurance are now part of our national pattern, and there is little doubt among the experts that this movement will continue to spread during the next few years. So it is in almost every area of life.

In the field of education, for example, the influence of the state is being felt. Not only is there the probability of some federal supervision, through a cabinet member and a greatly strengthened national bureau or department of education, but within the individual states of the Union, the supervision from the state capital is increasing rather than diminishing. This trend again had its supreme illustration in the world war; schools, colleges and universities—and in some instances, even seminaries—seemed to be instruments for the government to use in creating the particular talents it needed. The prescribing of particular courses of study in one subject or another by pressure, either direct or indirect, is growing apace, even with the abating of the war fever.

It is hardly necessary, however, to continue this catalogue; the subject has been covered, very adequately, in Paul Hutchinson's book *The New Leviathan*. What is not always realized, however, is that these facts and many like them point in one direction: the pattern of American life, whatever may be our particular personal wishes, is increasingly taking on a corporative quality. In economic and social fields, this is plain enough; it is as much true in agriculture as in industry. The educational field is not immune from the general trend; and the religious world is facing similar change.

That is the fact. The explanation of the fact, or rather the cause of it, is not so easy to set down. Roughly, it may be said that the extraordinary economic interdependence of the several nations, coupled with industrial expansion that makes it necessary for raw materials to be imported or exported from one country to another, has had most to do with the matter. Associated with this has been the rapid development of means of communication and travel, so that today's events in India, for example, have repercussions in the United States tomorrow, whereas in an earlier age it would have taken weeks or months for them to be felt. As Wendell Willkie saw, the world is 'one world.' In our own country, the loss of the frontier as a real factor in our national life has brought us all together in one great family; here, too, we are utterly interdependent. As our population has increased, we have built up great cities requiring food and other supplies from rural sections, just as the country areas need that which the large industrial plants in or near the cities must provide. This economic and social interdependence is paralleled by a cultural interrelationship; no longer are there many varieties of culture in America. As we saw in our discussion of the changed American scene, there is a uniformity of outlook that is bound to bring about a uniformity of behavior pattern. And since we all tend to behave alike, think alike, feel alike, desire alike, and will alike, we have become a unity with an overwhelming weight of mass authority and a strong tendency to smother the individual in that mass.

There is another consideration that is profoundly important. Our interdependence and interrelationship have led to a concern for social justice. We cannot afford to permit some men to assert themselves in such a way that they deny the rights of others to live healthy and happy lives; we are shocked at the consequences of industrial exploitation; we are impelled to ask for security in employment and comfort in old age for those who work for us. Nor is that all; those who are performing the essential work of the nation insist that they be given the right to work, to good housing, to decent wages, to a secure old age. They demand a share in the profits of their employers, as well as working conditions that are healthy and safe.

Furthermore, the series of depressions that the modern economic situation has produced and individualistic economy failed to meet, forced us to take steps toward control from which there has never been a retreat. Although much of the legislation under the 'New Deal' was declared unconstitutional, its major controls have remained in the programs of all progressive parties, and many of its achievements have been retained; or were reintroduced because of the war. There have been countless influences and forces that have brought about the present movement; it is difficult to see any way in which that movement, once started, can be brought to a halt; and very few right-thinking people would wish this to happen.

The result is that the dominant drive in our country is in the direction of greater planning and supervision. It is the same everywhere else in the world. Soviet Russia is the 'horrible example' for many ultraconservatives; but there is no European country, even those still struggling to be democratic, like Great Britain or France, in which the movement is not the same as that in America. The only difference is that in most other countries the movement is farther advanced.

We are bold to affirm that the pattern of life in America within a measurable period of time will be predominantly 'totalitarian.' That word is not popular; it suggests the horrors of Nazi Germany or the state socialism of Soviet Russia, both of which seem to most Americans to be equally undesirable. But what actually we mean is control by governmental agencies of the life of the people—a control that can be thoroughly democratic in spirit as easily as it can be militaristic, racial, or partial in terms of class. The emerging social system in America, the new society appearing in this land, will be collectivist. Whether it will also be democratic or something else depends upon what we do about it. The real danger is that we shall be so slovenly and indifferent in our attitude, so ready to practice a policy of *laissez-faire,* that we shall permit a monopolistic or even militaristic clique to control the life of the nation. Our tremendous opportunity is to see to it that the 'common man' is at the center of the picture, and that American democracy evolves from individualism into a planned society in a way that will safeguard all that is best in the free traditions of this nation.

Something must now be said about the situation in which religion finds itself, or will find itself, in such a planned society.

The present tendency to regard any and all religion as important mainly because it gives a certain sanction to society will doubtless continue and even increase in influence. We do not mean that the Church itself will welcome this stand, although there is the possibility that it may be strongly tempted to do so. The German Christians at first thought that they were doing Christianity a great service by relating it closely to the whole Nazi world view; as Mr. T. S. Eliot pointed out so wisely in a note printed at the back of his book *The Idea of a Christian Society,* much Christian teaching in Great Britain tended *mutatis mutandis* in the same direction. The situation is the same in America, and the Christian Church needs to be alert to the danger.

Not long ago the writer was present at the commencement exercises of one of the best preparatory schools in the United States. The speaker was a clergyman who occupies a famous pulpit in a great city. His address was a forceful one, heard with interest by the students and with enthusiasm by their parents and friends. The main emphasis of the speech was on the fact that if the graduates wished to be sound, patriotic, right-living citizens of this country, it was incumbent upon them to appreciate and utilize the insights of Christian faith. The Church, we were told, would help them to be strong men making their just contribution to national welfare; it would guarantee that our American 'way of life' would be preserved against all dangerous attacks from enemy nations. In a word, it boiled down to the admonition, which was not spoken by the minister but might just as well have been, that religion, and supremely the Christian religion, is the great sanction for our country and its ways. If one wishes to secure the future of these things, one must support the Church.

Such an address illustrates our point only too well. For the reverend gentleman was an honest and earnest man, whose intentions were excellent and whose goodwill was evident. He simply did not see what he was saying. He was making Christianity a *function* of our national life. He was implicitly denying its integrity and its supreme claim upon men's allegiance in *its own right,* and implicitly defending Christianity simply because it happens to be good and useful for the preservation of American ideals.

What he did unconsciously may one day be done quite consciously and intentionally. Indeed, it is already being done. One need only read the Monday morning newspapers to see how on the preceding day some of the clergy have committed themselves wholeheartedly to the proposition that the religion they preach is primarily concerned with securing the best interests of our national existence. And of course it *is* concerned with securing such interests; but not *primarily.* It is the adverb that denotes the danger.

When the new society has been established among us,

the danger will be all the greater. For that society will be concerned to see that all men have sufficient income, sufficient comfort, sufficient health, and all the other necessary sufficiencies of life, in order that they can realize to a fuller degree the intrinsic possibilities of human nature. This is all to the good. But precisely because it *is* so good and so important, so close to the heart of Christian concern for the rights of one's brothers, so intimately related to the compassion all Christians ought to feel, it will be the easier to confuse the preservation of that kind of society and the greater implementation of its quite real values, with the Christian religion itself. This is perhaps a credit to the hearts of those who make the confusion; it is certainly no credit to their heads. Nor does it indicate any very clear vision of the meaning of the historic faith, as it has come to us through the long tradition of the Christian Church. The confusion is very real indeed. We ought to be able to see it and make the necessary important distinctions; but there is evidence that many leaders will be too blind to do so.

The chaplains in the armed services seem frequently to fit into this pattern; religion is used as a morale-builder, necessary to maintain the sound character and fighting qualities desired in soldiers and sailors. Unhappily this kind of mentality has extended more widely, as there are many pastors who seek to commend Christianity solely on the ground that it is an inherent part of 'the American way of life.' In effect, this means that the Christian faith and the Christian Church are reduced to the position of being adjectival to a greater substantival reality, which is the life of the nation itself. Such an idea is not unlike that view of religion we have seen supported by thinkers like John Dewey (although with him it gets a more liberal tinge). It suggests implicitly the substitution of good citizenship for firm religious faith, and it has a specious appeal because it seems to combine patriotic support of our native land with the defense of the value of religion. The subtle shift from a religion that commands allegiance because it is true, to a religion that is proffered as an invaluable bolstering for a mundane society, is not always noticed.

An illustration of how this may be done is given when agencies of the government take over the religious instruction of citizens in the so-called 'non-sectarian' religious teaching that has been inaugurated under army auspices for newly enlisted men. Some months ago, a newspaper item reported that such teaching had been so 'successful' at Fort Knox, where the experimental Universal Military Training Camp was maintained, that it had been extended more widely among recruits in the armed forces. With this situation as a beginning, it requires little imagination to see ways in which, in the new society, the children of the land may be given some sort of 'non-sectarian' instruction that will have for its ultimate object precisely what the army was prepared to say was the goal for its teaching of religion— the building of a high morale, or (as would undoubtedly be said if such instruction were given in the school system) the development of 'good citizenship.' The state would be using religion for its own purposes, with the intention of developing a type of man. Religion would be adjectival, the state and its ideal the substantive. Nor is this particular illustration the only one that may be adduced; in community after community, pressure is being brought upon the schools to introduce some sort of 'non-sectarian' teaching, of a religious and moral nature, into the regular school curriculum.

It is our opinion that with the tremendous expansion of governmental controls in the new society now emerging, this field of educational control of religion will be expanded *pari passu*. The very heart of the danger is that in each instance the movement will have excellent intentions, will be blessed by those who are most idealistically minded, will be approved even by many religious leaders, and so will seem to be only the right development of an already present concern that men and women should be given the most thorough training for citizenship and social ideals.

Another characteristic of the 'new society' is that almost inevitably it is destined to have a 'this-world' perspective. Nor is this unconnected with the prevalent state of mind in America during the past quarter-century. We have seen that one aspect of the culture of our own time is its dominant secularism—that is, its almost unconscious limitation of the horizon of life to what may be seen and heard about us in the realm of time and space. In reaction from an excessive 'other-worldliness,' religion itself has taken to confining its interests largely to the present world of our experience; this is one reason why 'personality adjustment,' often in terms of contemporary society or at best in terms of some ideal society contemplated by the religious mind,

has become the substitute for a more deep-rooted notion of 'salvation,' consonant with the general tradition
of the Christian centuries.

Americans today, unless they be remarkably untrue
to type, are not likely to spend much time worrying
about 'eternity' or (as they would probably describe it)
'the future life.' They are much more concerned with
'getting things done'; or, if they have gone beyond that,
they are interested in the good 'they can do here and
now.' This surely is not an unworthy ambition, but it
is necessary to notice that it has meant a fairly thorough
obscuring of what we might term 'the ultimate horizons
of life.' The cosmic perspective of the average American and the use of such perspective to appraise behavior
or to judge the worth of some policy or program are
noticeable more by their absence than by any reinter-
pretation of the meaning of the old phrases.

This attitude of mind in our citizenry is in keeping
with the inescapable probability that a society organized explicitly to provide for the needs of the greatest
number of people will be a society so necessarily cen-
tered on this object that it will tend increasingly to disregard any other interests. That such a tendency can
lead only to a worship of the state is plain to us who
have witnessed the recent example of Germany under
the Nazi regime. But even if it does not reach the point
of state-worship—which, in any explicit sense, seems
thoroughly unlikely in America—it must mean that
little time will be left for the larger questions of human
destiny. A Christian would say 'this should ye do, and
not leave the others undone.' It is not the Christian,

however, who is determining the 'set' of the new order, but those who are so indeterminate in their religious allegiance and so incapable of recognizing the essential Christian point of view that they often feel they are certainly serving the cause of 'religion' when they are in effect merely substituting an orientation that is at the poles from traditional religious ideas. The best that can be hoped is that the new society will be governed by altruistic motives rather than sheerly materialistic ones—and, unless reactionary economic interests gain control, it is likely that some such idealism will mark society, with the kind of religious 'aura' to which we have already given some attention.

The fundamental problem in the new order will be the same as that we now confront, as far as the individual citizen is concerned. He will be given an increased number of gadgets, an increasingly mechanized existence, and more and more equipment to provide comfort and save labor. It is right that this should be, and nobody will wish to decry it. But the truth is that the more we have of this kind of thing—the more we are supplied with 'canned music,' manufactured entertainment, commercialized sports, and all that is in one way or another 'prepared' for us after the fashion of pre-digested food, combined with the use of more and more tools and appliances—the more we are likely to forget the fact that man is a limited and finite creature. Some one has remarked that 'while the heavens used to declare the glory of God, neon signs today proclaim the cleverness of man. . ." This situation points toward the appalling loss of any sense of the ultimate meaning of things, the final 'why,' in our contemporary culture; and it hints that in a society that spreads even more widely the 'comforts and conveniences of life,' the need to recognize and make terms with Reality will be less likely to crash up against men and women in their ordinary existence. It is here, however, that religion's 'otherworldly' note speaks to men. And it is here that an integral religion must be prepared both to challenge and to comfort man; for even in his self-satisfied secularism and as a member of a secular-minded society, man is not competent 'of himself to help himself.' He may realize this only at moments of crisis—bereavement, imminent death, the sense of utter frustration that sometimes comes over him—but at his deepest and best, as the poets have testified, he does realize it, knowing that the true story of each of us is that 'we look before and after; we pine for what is not; our sincerest laughter with some pain is fraught.'

It is probable that in the new society a tolerant attitude to all religions will be continued, provided they do not seem to contradict or imperil the values regarded as essentially American. But as soon as a religion begins to make claims running counter to these values, or insists on its right to criticize vigorously some national policy, that religion will be in danger of persecution. The persecution is not likely to be to the death; more likely it will resemble the treatment of such groups as the Jehovah's Witnesses during the war and thereafter. Or if such persecution does not appear, public opinion with its tremendous power will do the job; the dissenting religious group will be regarded as 'un-American' or 'unpatriotic,' and will be condemned on that ground as unfit for a hearing among us.

In the main, however, we may assume that religion, and especially Christianity, will be strongly approved. It is not only the reactionaries who talk about 'Christian standards'; it is quite as much the leaders of our progressive movements. What in another place the present writer has described as 'persecution by praise' is thus a very real danger. This can be brought about by the constant lauding of those intangibles called 'values,' 'principles,' and 'ideals,' which are supposed to be the truly important things about Christianity. The dogmas of the faith, the integral necessity of worship, the supernatural virtues of faith, hope, and charity, will be considered secondary or irrelevant.

Not only is talk about 'values, principles, and ideals' easier than insistence on dogma, worship, and the supernatural virtues; it is also much more in accord with that idealistic attitude of mind that expresses itself in our emphasis on 'our manifest destiny.' The ordinary man is not likely to see what has happened. On the one hand, he is not sufficiently integrated into the Christian tradition to understand its organic nature, while on the other he is so imbued with the spirit of American culture that he attaches to it a positively religious significance. So it is that, as the new society emerges, we shall find that it has a certain religious quality, related inevitably to the Christian terminology but, to a large degree, only an *ersatz*. What may then happen is that a sort of residuum of Christianity, when all the strong meat has been rejected, will be taken as the 'American religion.' It might very well be defined by some leader as 'the spirit of Christianity'; the body of the thing will have been left behind to 'moulder in the grave,' but the 'spirit,' so understood, may be accepted as essential and invaluable for our social life.

As the consequence of this process, the likelihood is that the Christian Church will exercise a diminishing influence on the American scene. It will undoubtedly continue to speak through commissions and conventions, but it will be heard only in the degree to which it accords approval to the accepted policy. Let the Church denounce or decry, and it will be rejected as too 'spiritual' or condemned as meddling where it should mind its own business. There is a danger, too, that the rise of the 'new orthodoxy' may cause some religious leaders to agree that it is not the Church's business to enter into the study of economic, social, industrial, and political problems and to make pronouncements on these subjects. Its job is religion; it should stick to that job.

Furthermore, religion may increasingly be patronized as a valuable instrument for the securing of mental health for the community. The judgment of many psychiatrists and psychotherapists, that religion is necessary to a sound and integrated life, is confirmed by the history of the human race; but it is dangerous when religion is regarded primarily as a therapeutic. The priest or pastor may be relegated to the role of a modern 'medicine man,' who steps in to assist in the adjustment of sick personalities, working with the physician and the psychiatrist toward this end. So relegated, he fits nicely into the pattern, for then his job, like that of his colleagues in therapy, is to secure that men and women shall be properly adjusted to life in society. Once again, religion is made adjectival to the social system. If a theologian affirms, in anything like the thoroughgoing fashion often advocated, that man ought not to be adjusted to the social pattern, he may be told that he is not 'abreast of the times.' Yet there is a sense, as eminent experts in the field of psychosomatic medicine have agreed, in which man is not truly man unless he has tensions and conflicts with his social environment and even within his own personality; they see that the only perfectly adjusted man is, either literally or figuratively, a dead one. Acceptance of religion simply as a means toward social adjustment and mental health may very well turn out to be a subtle but effective method for putting it in its place in a society that wishes to control every aspect of man's being for the social ends it approves. That way lies fascism—and it was not so long ago that Aldous Huxley gave us his terrible picture of a *Brave New World.*

Along with the dangers and evils that lurk in the new society and in the attitude that may be taken in that society toward Christianity and religion in general, there is much that is good. The new society will mark the appearance of an order of things in America in which it is quite likely that the 'common man' will be accorded a larger measure of his human rights. We believe that the progressive forces are more certain of winning the day than those that would drive us into an American version of fascism. Men like Henry Wallace, so easily

dismissed as 'crackpots' by the defenders of special privilege and the militaristic war lords, have shown that
they can win a tremendous following. The American
populace is still idealistically inclined, with all of the
perils of that spirit and with all of its values. There is
genuine good will in the ordinary citizen, a sense of
decency and fair play.

We do not wish to suggest that the new society, even
if it cares for the 'common man,' will be without its real
liabilities and dangers; these are inevitable in any
corporative system. Neither do we wish to intimate that
there could ever be a *perfect* social structure in a world
that is finite and among men who are sinful. But if there
is more to be said for a society in which the controls of
government are exercised to prevent the accumulation
of wealth by a few than there is for a disordered society
in which 'free enterprise' runs riot and millions are im-
poverished or degraded, Christianity has a stake in the
new society and eagerly awaits its appearance. Its place
may be hard to maintain in that society, the attitude
taken toward it may be wrong, the struggle to preserve
the Church's integrity may be difficult, but the Christian who believes that God wills that *every* man should
have as abundant a life as is possible for *any* man, will
work toward that end by supporting the movement
that seeks to swing the emerging order in a democratic
and liberal direction. He will not talk of it as if it were
just another example of man's sinful pretension. It is
here that we must guard against the danger of suppos-
ing that because in God's sight all men are sinners and
all human action partakes to some degree of the nature

of sin, it is all of a piece. There are ups and downs; there are more and less sinful actions as there are better and worse men. And societies may more adequately or less adequately reflect the will of God for his children.

With this in mind, we can say confidently that the emerging new society, if it takes the turn we believe it will take, is a better society than the one that has crumbled about us. It will have its perils for the Church, but it will at the same time offer men an opportunity to live more humanly and happily and healthily. For that reason, there need be no ambiguity in our attitude; we can welcome it heartily. But we need constantly to be on guard lest it become, in itself, what Dr. Tillich has called *demonic*. We must watch lest the inevitable 'totalitarianism' of such an order becomes an end in itself and thus arrogates to itself the loyalties that belong to God alone. Every social system has evils. That of the older individualism was the claim, made for the individual man, to rights and prerogatives that cannot be his, for they are only God's. It tended to think of each man as 'master of his fate' and 'captain of his soul.' The evil of the new society is that it may put Leviathan in place of God, attributing to the state the rights and prerogatives that belong to God alone.

It is for the Church, furthermore, to exert its influence, wherever it may be exercised and however slight its power, and to insist on the value of the person as well as on the necessity for his social life; to demand, as far as it can make itself heard and felt, that just as in the older individualism social claims had to be recognized, so in the newer planned society personal claims must be given their due. The Church's task is to bring to men a gospel that offers them a footing in eternity and gives meaning to their life on earth. All of the possible dangers to the Church that we have discussed in this chapter, in so far as they bear upon the religious aspect of the new society, may be summed up by saying that Christianity may be viewed as too much a this-worldly religion, tempted to confine its message to the life of man in society and to use its gospel as a means of satisfying men with temporal existence.

We are far from thinking that Christianity is nothing but an 'otherworldly' religion. Enough has been said in previous chapters to make that clear. Yet there is a primary emphasis on the supernatural in Christianity, the supernatural that penetrates and pervades the natural, and gives meaning and value to it. It is by no society, however controlled for the good of the 'common man,' that the broken hearts of God's children will finally be healed. The gospel the Christian Church is commissioned to preach is profoundly concerned that this world shall be a fit *via* for the sons of men who by the Incarnation have been made the brothers of God the Son. It must support every effort to bring rich and full life, in this present world, to the men and women and children who walk its ways. But, in loyalty to itself, it dare not rest there. Its primary stress is on eternal destiny, which is not so much beyond this world in point of time—that is, after death—as it is above and yet in this world at every moment of time. Here and now, as men live in a world of flux and flow, they are to be related to their true homeland and to find their rest in God. Without this, they are, in the long run, frustrated and hopeless, however superficially happy they may be. For God has set eternity in men's hearts.

The full gospel of the Church of Christ cannot be preached unless all of this be in it. The Church must see to it that, in any and every way possible, it speaks to men of their true nature as God's sons. Its main interest is not that they be good citizens, although it may very well bless them as they try to live as such, but that they be good men, who have had poured into them a grace that dignifies life, here and now, and opens up the possibility of 'continued growth in God's love and service' hereafter. That is why the Church must be true to its gospel—and true to itself, for the Church is, in the world of space and time, the imperfect yet actual presence of the eternal order of charity. In other words, the Church must not lose its own identity in the world of tomorrow.

What, then, is the best strategy for the Church? What ought it to do in a planned society? What is its place, properly speaking, in the new order that is making its appearance among us? It is to questions of this sort that we shall devote the next chapter.

6] *The Church in the New Society*

The Christian Church, in all of its communions, has been so linked with the society which is now in decay that many critics, among them loyal members of Christian bodies, are afraid the Church will be unable to survive the destruction of that society and the emergence of a new one. We cannot concern ourselves here with such a question—although it is a very real and profoundly serious one. We may be certain, however, that there will be vast changes in the future, perhaps in the near future, in the organization of the Church. Nobody has ever held that the national headquarters and the bureaucratic arrangements of Christian communions have anything to do with the divine rights and the divine nature attributed to the Church. Even Roman Catholics are hardly intent on claiming that the curia in Rome, with its reflection in the particular ecclesiastical organization in this country, is divine; the claims made for the Pope and for the institutional aspect of the Roman communion are on vastly different lines.

We shall simply recognize here that the organization of the Church may be profoundly modified in the next generation or two, as necessity demands. And we shall also take it for granted, and even welcome the fact, that the financial support of the Church will very shortly be on a different basis: no longer shall we be able to expect that heavy endowments, large gifts from the wealthy, investments of various kinds, and similar sources of income will be the means by which the Church's work is carried on. This change is already taking place for the inescapable reason that the wealthy are no longer so wealthy and that endowments and investments do not produce the returns that at one time were assured. The support of the Church is increasingly from the free and, on the whole, small contributions of the many who are devoted church people, rather than from a few rich well-wishers or from funds left by those who supported it in the past. A single example may be given to make this plain: our theological seminaries, in all denominations, are now more and more counting upon annual appropriations from parishes, dioceses, and similar sectional divisions, or upon the annual gifts of individual communicants, rather than upon the legacies that previously had been the principal source of their income. The Episcopal Church, with its 'Theological Education Sunday,' has been a leader in this new movement; and within a few years, it has found it possible by this means to raise many thousands of dollars to supplement the fast diminishing returns from investments.

To these matters we shall not advert. Nor shall we

have anything to say about the structural side of the
Church as the Body of Christ, about problems concerning Church government and Church order. Each communion has its own views on this matter. Some of them
—like the communion to which the writer belongs—have
an order associated with a specific kind of ecclesiastical
government and believed to be in some genuine sense
divine in origin and development. Other communions
have a type of order that they take to be 'convenient'
or valuable, but for which they make no more ultimate claims. But this kind of problem is not within
the scope of this book. Under whatever particular organization and with whatever administrative methods
and official agencies, it is likely that Christian groups
will continue for a long time with several traditional
orders, although we may hope that there may one day
be an agreed order that may bring together various
separated groups who have found ways by which differences can be reconciled in some larger unity. We are
here concerned with what might be called the larger
strategy of the Church as a whole, and with the particular expression of that strategy in given parishes and
congregations. We are concerned with the understanding of the Church's function in the new society as it
must be seen by those who profess and call themselves
Christians. In the large, our interest is in the relation
that should be sustained by the Church in regard to the
new society.

It is necessary first of all to embark on a theological
discussion, since it is essential that we know what the
Church *is* before we begin to talk about what the

Church should be and what the Church should do in the new society. Unhappily, this necessity is not always realized—and that is a comment on the way in which what we have called our American assumptions have eaten into Christian thinking. Far too frequently we seem to be content to skip a consideration of the essential nature of the Church and to plunge, without hesitation, into a strategy—with the result that we tend, often enough, to get nowhere very fast.

The Church, as we shall think of it in this chapter, is a divinely established organism, best described by the term 'the Body of Christ.' Although it has a history that may be studied by scientific methods, it is not exhausted by a human description; literally, there is more here than meets the eye. The Church is the organic reality in which Jesus Christ is at work in his world. This is not simply a 'high church' Anglican view; it is accepted by orthodoxy of every description and is indeed the only doctrine of the Church that can be said to have 'ecumenical' approval. The Church is not an accidental institutional phase in the Christian religion; it is integral to it, so much so that one may rightly say, 'No Church, no gospel.'

There are many ways in which this central understanding of the nature of the Church is verbally stated and visibly expressed in Christendom. But historically there has never been any doubt, except among eccentric groups, of the fundamental position. In America, however, the fact of the matter is that a sense of the Church as the Body of Christ has dropped from the consciousness of vast numbers of loyal church people, who tend to regard it as an association of persons bound together by common views and seeking a common end. This 'low' conception of the Church is not accepted by any reputable theologian. When, a few years back, the editor of *The Christian Century* called the Christian community 'the carrier of salvation,' we had reached a point where, even among extreme Protestants, the necessity and centrality of the Church was once again realized and emphasized.

Hence in our discussion we shall think of the Church as a group of men and women whose unity is not secured only by the fact that they are all 'followers of Jesus' or all believe in 'the Christian way of life.' We shall mean an organic unity, in which the life and work of the Lord Jesus Christ, God-made-Man, is continued in the world, so that succeeding generations may enter into relationship with him and may be employed by him for his own purposes. And we shall mean this without for a moment denying the sin, weakness, and error that obviously mar the Church as we see it about us. To this question of the Church's fallibility and yet divine nature, we cannot devote further attention; perhaps the writer may be permitted to refer the reader to an earlier book, *His Body the Church,* for a treatment of the problem of the imperfection of what he there calls the 'empirical Church' in relation to the indefectibility of what he calls the 'actual Church.'

As the Body of Christ, the Christian Church has about it those marks belonging to Christ himself: that is, it is 'one, holy, catholic, and apostolic.' It is one in that it partakes in and expresses the union of God and man accomplished in the incarnate Lord, binding those who are his members into a unity with one another in him. It is holy in that it is 'separated' from the world— that is, from human society and human affairs as they are organized in independence of God and his will—in order that it may bring God's supernatural charity to bear upon that world; as such, it produces in its members 'the fruits of the Spirit,' the holiness that comes from their common participation in the life of Christ. It is catholic in that it is an organism in which worship, faith, and common life are integrated; it is catholic in that its gospel and its mission are universal in significance, without regard to race or nation or class or to other differences between men, and with a capacity to bring to all who will accept it the saving grace of God in Christ. It is apostolic in that it is grounded in historical fact, culminating in the life and teaching and death and resurrection of Christ, in whom God, in a decisive manner, took action for the salvation of men in the sheer concrete fact of particular events; it is apostolic in that it is 'sent,' as the Greek word itself would suggest, to preach that gospel of God's saving action to all the world.

Into membership in that Body of Christ those who are by baptism united with the Church are received. They become, through that sacramental initiation, 'very members incorporate in the mystical Body of Christ, which is the blessed company of all faithful people.' This sense of membership in the Church as the Body of Christ has come alive in our day through the 'liturgical movement' in the Roman Catholic and

Anglican Communions and through the 'ecumenical movement' in Protestant Christianity, a movement in which Anglicanism has also had its share. To be a Christian means to be a member of the Body of Christ; or, as St.. Paul put it, to be 'in Christ' means that one is a partaker of the divine life which flows through Christ's Body and is conveyed to those who are united with its life. It is this lifting of men and women to the level of life 'in Christ,' to the 'engraced' life, to participation in 'God-Manhood,' that explains the real significance of the Church; apart from this it would have little significance beyond that of any society for religious and ethical culture.

It is unfortunately true that there is too often a failure among Christians to implement the richness ot this fact. It is for this reason that the Church seems an uninteresting, dull, and unimportant accessory to the Christian religion. But if the Church is to have any place whatever in the new society, it must first of all come to a fuller self-realization; as the late Archbishop Temple said, 'Let the Church *be* the Church.' If the Church is contented simply to be a human society and to act as such, without realization of its true nature, it will become precisely what, as we suggested in the last chapter, secular society may well wish the Church to be—the sanction for social order or the means of securing a certain religious quality for the new society, with almost complete acquiescence in every aspect of that society and with no integral and personal nature of its own.

The theological considerations we have just adduced

have a deep significance for us. For the first necessary step in the Church's strategy is that it become conscious of *itself*. Without a strong self-consciousness—that is, without an awareness of what the Church really and essentially *is*—all of our work will be on mistaken lines. The Church must be sure that no matter what approval or disapproval may be given it, no matter what praise or contempt it may receive, no matter how it may be esteemed or disesteemed, it never loses sight of its own true nature. It is the Body of Christ, alive and active in the world until the consummation of God's purpose in history.

By liturgy and by preaching this awareness is cultivated. It is stimulated by liturgy, the public worship of the Church as its members gather themselves together for the adoration of God through Jesus Christ his Son our Lord; it is proclaimed in sermon, as the members of the Church hear 'the Word of God preached.' Most of all, however, it is expressed and made manifest in the common life of the Church. It is here that the weakness of the Church in our contemporary situation is so evident. No matter how admirably the Church may express in its liturgical worship the fact of its being the Body of Christ, and no matter how eloquently this may be proclaimed in sermons, there will be little likelihood of its making any marked impact either upon the world outside the Church or even upon those who are nominal members, unless there is the continuous sense of corporate life in the Body of Christ as the central reality in the day-by-day living experience of Christian people. We cannot claim, with any confidence, that this is true today. The absence of that 'sense of belonging' to the Body of Christ is, to a large degree, the explanation of the much-criticized 'impotence' of Christianity in our modern world; and it will also be the explanation of the Church's continued impotence in the world of tomorrow. It is the task primarily of the individual parish and congregation to awaken this sense of a 'corporate belonging,' for unless the reality of membership in the Body of Christ is apprehended on these relatively 'lower' levels, it will never be apprehended in the wider 'ecumenical' Church. But how is this to be done?

It is in this connection and to meet this need that the strategy of 'cells' is important. We are advocating nothing original; the idea has been advanced frequently enough and with sufficient argument and emphasis, in many places and by many different writers. But we are convinced that it is the most important step toward securing that the Church shall have a genuine place in the new social order; and when that order has emerged, it will be essential that such 'cells' be in existence. Here is the task that must be given 'priority' in our thinking and planning.

What is a 'cell'? It is a group of convinced Christian believers, bound together by a dominant loyalty to the Christian Church's faith and its divine purpose, and so conscious of this loyalty that it pervades their life and thought. Such a group of Christians is what every parish or congregation is meant to be: it is, as St. Paul would have said, the Church, in Corinth or Athens or Ephesus, in Alameda or Tallahassee or Barre. There is nothing esoteric in the conception; it is, in fact, a way of saying that in each and every place where there is a body of Christians, they must be knit into a strong self-conscious group, aware of their function in the world, ready to give themselves to their task as Christians, and co-operating in every respect so that they may most adequately accomplish the work they are given to do.

A 'cell' is a congregation or parish in which the members have come to that self-awareness, and by so doing have come also to a recognition of their obligations as members of the Body of Christ in their particular locality and time. This means that they are dedicated as a group, and not simply as individuals, to the truth and necessity of the Christian faith. When they stand up to recite the creed, they are not simply joining in the statement of a faith that each of them happens to hold, but are uniting in a common affirmation of Christianity and their common acceptance of it. It means also that they understand that their meeting for worship is not a session in which each seeks to obtain help for his own life, but a common action in which the internal reality of the Body of Christ is given external expression. They could adopt the words of St. Augustine, referring to the offering of the Eucharist, that 'they offer what they are, they become what they offer.' For this reason, the Eucharist is the most expressive action of the Church, because it is the Church at work in its great task of realizing the truth of the gospel in worship, so that God may rightly be given the glory and his people adequately empowered for their Christian living in the world of space and time. To be a member of a 'cell' in the Body of Christ means that the believer, along with his fellows, is opening his whole personality to the health-giving life of Christ himself, and, in so far as he is able, is seeking to be the instrument through which that life flows out into the world in the particular sphere in which he happens to be situated, in work and play. To the 'cell' in a given town or country area, the Christian returns for strength and refreshment; from it he goes out to carry its influence to the world that is not christianized. This is the function of a parish or congregation; this is the meaning of a Christian 'cell.'

Nothing like this understanding of the purpose of the local congregation has permeated the minds and hearts of Christian people in our day. Yet, humanly speaking, it is upon this kind of understanding that the future of the Church in the new society would appear to depend; if it is to have any place in the world of to-morrow, this is the place it must have. The vivid realization of this vocation will lead to enormous changes in the program of any parish that is about its business, for it will mean that every aspect of the congregation's life, the preaching, services of worship, community welfare work, and the many other activities and interests that take up so much of the time and energy of the typical congregation, will be reoriented in the light of a new conception. Nothing that is good need be altered in content, but a wholly new spirit will enter into the life of a congregation that is thoroughly conscious of the stupendous fact that *it* is a 'cell' in the Body of Christ, with the vocation to *be* Christ to the particular community in which it is set.

Since one of our major tasks is to correct and, where

need be, combat the non-Christian assumptions and presuppositions of secular and of semi-Christian society, the congregational 'cell' must be sure that in its own life it expresses, as far as possible, the essential spirit of the Christian faith. The Christian 'mind' can be most fully developed—indeed, it cannot be otherwise developed—by actual concrete living together on Christian assumptions. For this reason, the life of the Church as concreted in a given locality can no longer be the rather precious and specialized existence of groups of like-minded people united for religious interests. The 'cell' must be drawn from all ranks and classes of society, and no special privilege can be allowed to find place within it. The notion of 'class churches,' even if these be of 'the working-classes,' is abhorrent. Guilds and organizations must be planned on the corporate basis of Christian fellowship, rather than on mere personal interest and liking. The same spirit must permeate every aspect of parish life, no matter how this may offend the socially prominent or those who like to think of themselves as intellectually gifted or officially superior. This idea is often accepted as a generality but it must find its actual expression in the 'cell.'

Teaching in the parish must be oriented about Christian 'belonging.' And it must be directed toward the building of a Christian 'mind' among those who call themselves by the Christian name. There seems to be no escape from the necessity for parochial schools of one sort or another. As the secular educational system takes over increasing areas of the life of its students, the Christian Church must insist upon its right and upon its duty to educate its children. Whether this will mean that the Church will set up in each community a school for the children of Christian parents, or whether it means that some arrangement will be effected whereby sufficient time is somehow secured for a strong and vigorously prosecuted program of Christian nurture in addition to the secular system, parochial education is a vital necessity. It is very likely—and to the writer it seems inevitable—that we shall be forced very soon to contemplate ways in which particular congregations or groups of congregations having similar beliefs can establish and maintain primary and secondary schools that will have at the heart of their curriculum the truths of Christianity and their implementation in behavior. In the new society, when it finally emerges, this step may be so necessary that humanly speaking the Christian Church will be unable to continue without it. The Roman Catholic system of parochial education need not be our model; but some definite parochial educational program must be established.

The amount of religious instruction that can be given in the conventional church school or Sunday school is not enough to help the children develop an attitude of mind, a set of assumptions, and an orientation toward life that can balance the secularized outlook and the humanistic assumptions that even now dominate the life of the nation and will dominate it increasingly in the future. Our religious educators have laid upon the church schools an enormous task that they must meet with every talent and resource they possess. If the Christian youth of the land is to know its Christian calling, it must learn it from the earliest years. This will imply a second point in the educational enterprise of the Church—a deepening of interest in family teaching, and an insistence through sermon and instruction that the homes of Christian people must be *Christian* homes, rather than homes in which people who happen to be Christians happen to live.

The primary and secondary levels of education are not sufficient, however, even with the addition of a strong home influence exerted in a Christian direction. The nation must have leaders; and as Christians, we are concerned that these leaders, as far as possible, be Christian leaders. Indeed, this is the condition for preserving a society in which liberal and democratic ideas, in the right sense of those words, are predominant. The tendency toward a purely secular and humanistic outlook produces results that we saw only too well in the spectacle of a nation like Germany, that went 'all out' for the development of leaders, but produced those who, while they were greatly gifted, were perverted in their outlook and hence easy victims of a totalitarianism of race, blood, and state, with its appalling militaristic accompaniments. The writer with his friend Dr. T. S. K. Scott-Craig, has already endeavored to argue in a little 'manifesto on the Christian college,' entitled *The College Militant,* for consciously Christian institutions of higher learning; it seems a transparent fact that without such institutions, supported financially and morally by the Christian Church, we face the danger of a society that is not merely 'neutral' toward the Christian understanding of life and human destiny, but may become, in the long run, positively inimical to that understanding.

Education, however, is only part of the interest of the Christian 'cell.' The development of a sense of the meaning of Christian 'appurtenance,' to use von Hügel's word, is the prime concern. Christian worship is the essential means to that development. In the early days of the Church, as Dom Gregory Dix has shown in *The Shape of the Liturgy,* Christians came together for worship for a very particular reason. They congregated not because they would be present at attractive meetings of like-minded people, nor because they wished to enjoy the opportunity for personal spiritual communion with Christ their Lord. The former could be had in many other ways, while the latter was open to any individual Christian at any time and in any place. They came together because it was 'meet, right, and their bounden duty' so to do; because in this way they realized and made into concrete actuality their common life as Christians. A Christian who did not come to the public worship of the Church—which was, of course, the Christian Eucharist—was by absence proclaiming himself to be not genuinely a Christian; he was 'excommunicated,' either by reason of his own sin against the community or because he did not wish longer to continue in its fellowship. This way of understanding the meaning of Christian worship has been lost by us in these latter days, when people go to church because they happen to like the service or because they enjoy the sermon or because they have a predilection for the type of music rendered.

A 'cell' in the Body of Christ will realize its nature when it is met together for worship—above all and uniquely when it is met together to plead the sacrifice of Christ as it is re-presented in the offering of the Eucharist from Sunday to Sunday. The sacrament of the Lord's Supper, so conceived, is no optional matter. Both Luther and Calvin wished it held each Sunday. The members of the denomination called the Disciples of Christ, quite as much as 'high Church' Episcopalians, Roman Catholics, and Eastern Orthodox, have seen this central truth and have acted upon it. In itself, of course, the Lord's Supper will not accomplish the task of making the Body of Christ a reality, for there must be the further externalization that carries that Supper and its deepest meaning into day-by-day living; but without the Lord's Supper, the sense of common membership in the Body, with the full grasp of the significance of that membership, is not possible. It is for this reason that we must welcome the growing emphasis on worship, and especially upon the Holy Communion, as the peculiarly significant Christian action. In the world ahead of us, this will be doubly important, for unless there is some strong bond of unity, such as the Lord's Supper creates by its divinely given sanction, it is impossible to see how the Christian community can continue to be the self-conscious community of men and women corporately committed to Christ and intent upon being his instruments in the world.

Stemming from this strong core in Christian worship, the 'cell' is to reach its members in all of the exigencies of their common life. The occasions of birth, marriage, and death are obvious enough, and to them the Church has always given rightful attention. But it must make more of entrance into Church membership by baptism, which instead of being a 'hole-in-the-corner' affair should be the glad welcoming into the Christian life of another human being who is thereby made a Christian and given the potentialities of Christian discipleship. Family events, such as anniversaries of marriages or birthdays, must be celebrated by the parish in whatever may seem appropriate ways. In every manner possible, it must be the duty of the given 'cell' to create a sense of 'belonging' and a joy in that fact, on the part of every member of the Body of Christ, as well as to manifest the common sharing in that membership and the common concern for all aspects of the life of every believer, so that it becomes a matter of sheer experience that 'each lives in the other and all live in Christ.'

Adult Christian training is another element in the program of the 'cell.' Just as the communists today have their meetings for learning more about the ideology of their party, so the Christian parish must have its ways by which those who are convinced in allegiance may together explore the implications of that allegiance. This is how the Christian 'mind' can be developed among older people. It is also the way each can come to understand that to be a Christian means to be a person different from the ordinary run of citizens, with standards and principles that are not identical with those of 'any good man,' and with demands laid upon him such as are not even envisaged by the typical American of 'good will.' Tomorrow will not be a time to blur the lines that distinguish the Christian from others; it will be a time to make those lines sharper, even while the Church insists and teaches that the Christian must appreciate the values and goods in secular thinking and acting, and above all must not withdraw himself from the world into a kind of haven of refuge where *he* is safe and others take the·road to the city of destruction.

We can envisage a program for parish meetings and training groups in which personal problems like those concerning family life and marriage, sexual relationships, as well as social questions, like the relation of Christian faith to business and professional work, the will of God in economic and national affairs, would be considered. This sort of thing is, of course, already done to some degree in some places; the places, however, are too few and the approach is too often by way of discussion of problems without any appreciation of the light the developing Christian moral tradition throws upon them. Yet it is not only this ethical aspect of Christianity that should be taken into such meetings and studied by such groups. The meaning of the Christian faith and the significance of Christian worship are primary. The whole range of theology is open to the average believer, even though he may not be able to make much of the intricacies of historical theology. He can be helped to know and appreciate Christian doctrine as it relates to his own life and problems. The Christian 'cell' has before it an enormous opportunity in these and many related areas; it can do an extraordinarily effective piece of work in creating in the believer the Christian attitude toward his problems and those of society, and so can supplement or supplant the imperfections or perversities of the secular point of view commonly held (even by those who are Christian in profession and in desire).

Is the parish developing a Christian conscience on the various social problems that face the local and national and international communities? If it is not, it is derelict to its responsibility. In the new society, it will have a unique and positive contribution to make at this point. Quite apart from its ability to produce results, it can bring to bear upon these problems the Christian insight into the nature of man. In a given situation the parish will have its testimony to bear on such matters as housing, industrial strife, economic injustice, and the like, while in the new society as a whole it will have its work cut out for it to be heard on the safeguarding of the rights of personality and the liberty belonging to every man even in a social order designed to seek his best good. It will have its part, too, in larger matters, such as the relations between nations and the total world picture. By sermon and moral teaching as well as by study through the group method, the Christian witness in and to the world must be made plain, even when it appears (as well it may) that very little can be done to actualize what is implied in the Christian outlook.

This brings us to our final point, so far as practical measures are concerned. The Church must strengthen the life in prayer of all its communicants. This can be done at the parish level by small groups, not unlike the old Methodist 'class meeting'; it can also be done on a

wider scale by 'retreats,' held in convenient places at
many times during the year, when men and women—
and even children—can be taught how to pray, how to
develop more deeply the life of devotion, how to grow
in the knowledge of God through other than intellectual means. Bible classes and similar agencies may
be effective in the Christian 'cell'; larger gatherings to
consider Scripture and personal religion also have their
place.

But in season and out of season, it is *above all* the ob-
ligation of the Christian 'cell' to proclaim the gospel of
God in Christ. First of all, this must be done for those
who are already members of the church, lest they fall
into the attitude of thinking the Christian gospel easier
and less exacting than it is. In view of the tendencies
mentioned in our last chapter—the relegation of Christianity to a sanction for the social system or a matter
of individual taste—it is incumbent upon the Church
to make known to its members the all-comprehending
nature of the gospel, and to see that it is understood by
Christian people that the faith cannot be reduced to
an ethical system or to any other *ersatz* for a supernatural religion. Far and away too many loyal church
people, or those who would at least lend their support
to the Church if they were somehow stimulated to do
so, think of Christianity in terms that are, in the long
run, secularistic and humanistic. Preaching and teaching must be along lines that will correct this misunderstanding, and make the gospel once again what it has
ever been—the saving news of God's action for men in
Christ, establishing a new relation to him that gives

meaning to present existence and opens a life that can persist through death.

To those not in the Church, there is also a message to be given. The gospel must be proclaimed as more important than the good citizenship their country demands of them. It must be presented boldly and flatly as a *gospel*, with supernatural sanctions. Here the newer 'orthodoxy' of our day is doing the work it ought to do, even if it does not manage to find points of contact that will open for the outsider new possibilities of hearing the gospel and of coming to terms with it. Missionary work in the particular community in which the Christian 'cell' is located, as well as in wider fields at home and abroad, remains a necessity. The Church dare not become a satisfied community of those already convinced or on the way to being convinced; it must let its truth be known outside the fellowship and must find ways, appropriate to the given situation, for reaching as many people as possible through as many means as are available—through all kinds of activities that will have for their principal purpose the bringing of men and women into contact with their fellows who are Christian by conviction and affiliation.

The writer does not need to be told that he has suggested an enormous program for the Church. He is aware of this, as he is also aware of the fact that he has only been able to indicate certain aspects of the work that must be undertaken in the new society, as a particular congregation faces its situation. But some such new approach, along the lines of local development, seems to him the first essential. But there is more to be said, for while the local situation is of particular importance, the national scene is not without importance.

Part of the Church's task and opportunity will be in the support and further development of educational institutions, especially on the college level. This we have already suggested. Still another undertaking will be the establishment of schools for study, both for clergy and laity. The existence of such institutions as the College of Preachers in Washington and the School of the Prophets in San Francisco point this for the clergy; similar developments should be under way for the laity. Summer conferences have grown in numbers; there should be more of them. Regional schools of religion and institutes for religious life must be on the program of the Church. In all of these ways, the Church can be strengthened in its membership, so that those who are of the Body of Christ may be brought to know more fully what it means to be Christian and may become more ready to act in a fashion appropriate to their conviction. This will involve increased and constantly increasing co-operation between communions, so far as conviction permits.

The need, everywhere, is for an intensifying of Christian conviction. There was a time when the missionary work of the Church was primarily of an extensive sort. It was concerned with carrying the gospel to what were then called the non-Christian lands. Surely the missionary work of the Church in this direction must not be abated; but the time is upon us when we need to be sure that those who are already Christian are given a thorough grounding in the faith of the Church, in its worship, and in the demands and the helps it offers for daily life. Christianity has been spread so thin among us that we can hardly call America a Christian land, even in intention; it is 'neutral' if not pagan. In the new society, it is likely that this process will be accelerated, and if the Church is to have any vital place in that society it must deepen and intensify the membership it has. From that deepening and intensifying will come an extensive and diffusive influence, both in our national life and on other peoples. We have too long taken it for granted that we are well-rooted in the Christian way; in fact, we have been so slightly equipped in this direction that we are hardly able to recognize genuine Christianity when we see it.

In the over-all picture, what is the Church's place? The Church is to be in secular society an 'earnest' of the City of God, not identified with secular society nor yet so detached from it that it has lost all contact with it. The 'liberalism' of yesterday tended to merge Christianity with national life and interests; the newer 'orthodoxy' tends to make a complete divorce between them. Historic Christianity has seen the need for balance, and has insisted that while the Church is not part of secular culture or identified with the society surrounding it, it has its message and mission to that society. Its work is to bring the supernatural charity of God in Christ straight into the midst of the relative justice, if there be such, of the world, so that light and life may be generated for the sons of men. Among the changes and chances of this mortal life, even in the best of plans for their happiness and well-being, men and women are literally without hope if in this world only they have hope. It is to awaken them sharply to the eternal world, which permeates and penetrates this world, that the Christian Church speaks; it brings tidings from 'beyond the flaming ramparts of space and time,' but these are tidings that have a direct relevance to the affairs of space and time. It preaches a divine discontent, so that men may have the only enduring contentment—one that can face life and its trials, suffering and pain, death and its uncertainties, with a good courage and can emerge triumphant through a supernatural faith. Hence the work of the Church is unique and irreplaceable; no other agency can do it, for no other agency can claim to bring the forgiveness, the blessing, and the empowering of God to the daily life of men.

We may well believe that the Christian gospel will not have too wide a hearing or too general an acceptance in the world of tomorrow. But that does not imply that the Church's task is the less exacting. The Church has faced, before this, a world that was relatively indifferent if not actually hostile; it will be no new thing to ask the Church to face such a world once again. It is probable that the Church will have to do so, whether it wishes to or whether it abhors the responsibility. The future does not look rosy for organized religion; we should be deceiving ourselves if we thought it did. Religion in an 'airy' sense, or religion in a mundane sense, will doubtless have its day; but religion in the Christian sense, as understood by the historic Christian Church, may very well be in for a bad time. Let us accept this, if it be the fact; but let us continue our planning and work out our strategy so that the Church can carry on at its old job. If it succeeds, it may 'redeem the time' and have its reward in turning the new society into one that will become the carrier for a Christian faith that will bring the world much nearer to the will of God, much more satisfactorily the embodiment of his purpose for human life. If it cannot succeed in so christianizing the social order, it can at least give a central meaning and sense to the lives of some—many or few—who live in that order; it can carry through the new 'dark ages' until the time comes, if it be God's will, when an even newer society will emerge, in which there is again opportunity to mold life as the Christian Church was able to mold it in an earlier age. If even this should fail to come to pass, the Church will still have done its divinely given work in bringing the knowledge of God and his salvation to as many as will hear.

After all, we have no guarantee anywhere in the gospels that the Christian faith will soon win the entire world. It is a relatively modern idea that things are getting better all the time, so that in the end the whole world will become perfect . . . and then, presumably, become a freezing uninhabitable planet! No; our task is to do our work as we see it, when we see it; to leave the future to God and not to ask that what *we* think to be right shall necessarily come to pass. Neither are we to judge that any man, even among those who flatly reject the gospel, is necessarily condemned to 'outer darkness'; God has uncovenanted mercies and his grace will be sufficient for any who are true to *whatever* light has been vouchsafed them. So we shall be delivered both 'from faithless fears and from worldly anxieties,' as the Anglican Prayer Book so admirably expresses it. Our confidence will be not in the returns we may report, but in the God who empowers us for our task.

It is not likely that any actual physical persecution will be in store for the Christian Church in this land; the persecution, if such there be, will be 'by praise,' as we have intimated on earlier pages of this book. In any case, we may still make our own, as we face the future with its new society, the words the reformer Martin Luther wrote and that we can all say, whether we be Protestant or Catholic, because they are so profoundly true and speak so meaningfully to our situation in any and every time:

> *Let goods and kindred go,*
> *This mortal life also;*
> *The body they may kill,*
> *God's truth abideth still:*
> *His Kingdom is forever.*

We have said little about the Church's concern for the social pattern, nor have we alluded to the place and need for such labors as have produced statements like those of the Oxford Conference, just before the war, or the Delaware Conference, more recently. We are tak-

ing it for granted that the Church, in its several denominations or through some united agencies, will continue this extremely important work. It is imperative
that Christian scholars bring to bear upon our problems, in every field, the whole weight of their devotion
and their learning; it is also imperative that these
scholars present their findings to the Church at large
and to the world. But we do not believe that the
Church's principal task is in this direction. The primary responsibility of the Church is that it shall be, in
itself, a healthy organism, filled with the life and power
of the living and redeeming God, intent upon relating
men to that life and power, and intent also that they
shall then relate the life and power of God to their
given situation in this world. We do not wish to suggest that the Church or its leaders should withdraw
from interest in secular problems, nor do we deny that
there is a true sense wherein we can work toward a
christianizing of society. We must criticize what is
wrong in the social sphere, we must denounce evil and
injustice, we must speak out loudly and frequently for
the rights of men, and do everything in our power to
implement the gospel in these areas. But we shall have
lost the secret of Christianity if we do not make the
relationship of man with God the very heart of our
preaching and teaching, our worship and our life. This
is what the Christian Church can contribute, if it
comes to that; it is the Christian Church alone that can
make this contribution, and it would be tragic if in its
concern over secondary, although important, affairs it
lost sight of its *raison d'être*.

For men are 'lost'—that is an old-fashioned phrase, but the truth of it comes home anew to many in our day. Mr. Chesterton once said that men are strangers in this world,

> They lay their heads in a foreign land
> Whenever the day is done.

That, he pointed out, is because they are in fact seeking 'an older town than Eden, a taller town than Rome.' They are homesick for God, in whom they can find peace for their souls. Without this peace, their best-made plans are as nothing, and the most utopian society turns into a veritable hell. There is an 'otherworldly' note about all human life, sometimes striking us precisely at the moment when 'we're safest,' and sending us off with 'fifty doubts and fears.' Browning's words, just quoted, put the point as directly as Chesterton's. For deep down we know that we are seeking some 'city which hath foundations, whose builder and maker is God.'

The Christian Church has its peculiar message to give to men, which makes it different from any other religion. It is the affirmation that God, who made us and the world in which we live, has himself entered savingly into that world and has established a fellowship of charity, where men may find a security beyond anything the world can offer, but which at the same time vindicates and guarantees the good in the world far beyond anything that 'our occasions' may indicate. God entered the world that we might 'have life, and have it more abundantly'; he also entered the world that the life we now live may be irradiated with the light of eternity, and that we may thereby be prepared in this 'vale of soul-making' for a destiny that is illimitable, since it is nothing other than God himself.

Here, then, is the central mission of the Church: the proclamation of the gospel of God in Christ and the incorporation of men into the life of God brought into our midst in Christ. It is salvation from sin and the gift of newness of life. It redeems our immediacies and re-lates us to the ultimacies of existence. It is given adequate expression not in the old-fashioned 'liberalism' that took too light and easy a view of human life and compromised too readily with the world and its ways; nor yet in the 'new orthodoxy' that sometimes seems to be too one-sided in denial of the world, in emphasis upon the exceeding sinfulness of man, and in a remote God whose interest in our affairs seems only to redeem us 'in principle' from our sins but never to enrich us in our worldly habitation. The gospel of the Church is given the most adequate, though always imperfect, expression in classical Christian theology. Yet the gospel requires a constant rethinking of and reapplication to the new situations in which men find themselves, the new knowledge given them, the new insight they secure concerning themselves and their experience. In other words, a dynamic orthodoxy alone can look steadily at life, without fear and without defeat.

A dynamic and vital orthodoxy lives at the heart of Christianity, continuing fixed despite the variations of 'liberalism' and its 'neo-orthodoxy.' Such a living orthodoxy *is* the 'Catholic Faith,' stated in the great credal affirmations like the Nicene and Apostles' Creeds, expressed in the worship of the Church and especially 'enacted' in the pleading of the sacrifice of Christ as the Church joins in the Lord's Supper, and secretly moving in the hearts of believers as they seek to live like Christians in our finite and sinful world.

7] *The Need for a Dynamic Orthodoxy*

We have tried to sketch something of the contemporary situation, with special reference to certain of the basic common assumptions we discern in the American mind. We have considered the appearance of a new religious outlook, superseding the older 'liberalism' and much closer to historic Christian orthodoxy, even if it has its own dangers and inadequacies as well as its values. We have intimated that the social order is in process of severe modification, so that within a measurable number of years it will be our lot, whether we like it or not, to live in a planned society whose controls will increasingly cover almost every aspect of our secular existence. Finally, we have said something of the dangers facing the Christian Church in such a new environment; and we have sought to suggest a program and policy appropriate to the Christian community in the world of tomorrow, with emphasis particularly upon the parish level, since that is where the average Christian lives and where the Church most closely touches him.

At the conclusion of the last chapter, it was said that

157

the vital need in our own day, and in the new society emerging in America, is for a dynamic orthodoxy that will avoid the mistakes both of 'liberalism' and of the 'new orthodoxy.' We recognized, as honestly as we could, that it is not at all likely that this basic Christian theology—or indeed, that Christianity in any dress —will sweep the country and win all its citizens to professed Christianity. Yet at the same time we insisted that it is essential that the Church know what it is about, understand its faith in the light of historical development and with due account of the learning of our own day, and stand firmly on that faith, so that it may serve as a kind of living core for the new society and thereby bring both insight and power to those who are ready to listen to its gospel and accept it as the 'master-light of all their seeing.'

Our purpose in this final chapter is to say more about what we have chosen to call dynamic orthodoxy, identical with what historically has been termed 'the Catholic Faith,' but alert to the newer knowledge we now possess and adapted to a world whose outlook and orientation are different from that of the Fathers or in the Middle Ages. Such a dynamic orthodoxy is implicit, to greater or less degree, in the major Christian communions that have their place in our American life. The 'orthodox' revival of our own day has recalled many in these denominations from their flirtation with a 'liberalism' that often tended to reduce Christianity to 'another gospel.' It is our hope that the extremes to which this revival has sometimes gone will be modified by wiser theologians. In the result, we should then see a

Christian teaching recognizably one with the faith of the centuries. And when that happens, we may well begin to look for the day when the several Christian communions can be brought into a genuine unity, based on the historic Christian faith rather than on 'reductions' of it.

It is to the basic assertions of historic orthodoxy that we wish now to give our attention, with the special purpose of seeing how they may apply to our changed cultural situation and have bearing upon life in the new society.

The first great assertion of dynamic orthodoxy is the fact of God. But since the term 'God' has been patient of many interpretations, historic Christianity is not interested simply in the term but in what the term has denoted. This is the dependence of the whole created world upon one supreme, eternal Reality, who alone truly *is* and without whom there would be nothing else. The late Archbishop of Canterbury, Dr. William Temple, used to say that 'God minus the world equals God; the world minus God equals nothing.' Although in an earlier day it was sometimes thought there could be absolute proof of the 'existence' of God, we are today likely to say that such proof never arrives at God in the sense in which Christianity means God; it arrives only at a logical conclusion to an argument and lacks the vitality and religious quality that make the very word itself a significant reality. Therefore we should be much more inclined to regard the so-called 'proofs,' whether they be St. Thomas Aquinas's famous five or the modern philosophers' three, as pointers toward God or converging evidences for his existence, rather than sheer rational demonstrations. But that God *is,* and that he is the supreme dependability in things, upon whom all else hangs and from whom all else derives its limited finite existence, is at the heart of the Christian faith. Nor is it left there. This supreme, eternal Reality is pervasive of the entire creation. There is no 'absentee' element in his relation to the world; he acts in it and through it, sustaining it and using it for his purposes, with whatever limited freedom he may have allowed it. He is not a remote being, but is 'nearer than hands and feet'; yet he is unexhausted by his creation and remains in himself utterly inexhaustible. So, as the theologian would put it, he is both immanent and transcendent. Furthermore, Christianity insists that while God is far above and beyond anything that we may know as personality, there is in him that unity, integrity, self-awareness, and capacity for communication with others that we denote when we speak of one type of created life as 'personal' rather than as 'impersonal.' There is no quality of bare being about God; he is a rich, vibrant, living Being, whose life is so supremely unified and integrated, so purposive and living, so self-aware and communicable, that the very creation itself comes into existence as the result of his diffusive goodness and life—not by an unwilled necessity, since the unity and integrity of the divine Reality make any such thing an impossibility, but by the freely willed act of One who is supremely good and therefore gives himself toward the making of other objects through which his goodness may be expressed and upon which it may be bestowed.

It can at once be seen that this central affirmation of a dynamic orthodoxy has nothing to fear from scientific investigation, since such inquiry is only a tracing of the ways God has taken and is taking in creating and sustaining and working through his world. The scientist cannot find God, for God is not the kind of reality discoverable through a telescope or microscope or pointer-readings. God is known in the living awareness of personal relationship, if he is known at all. The scientist is able to trace the order and plan of nature; and even though he finds no scientifically observable divine Reality, he finds the marks of an integrating, whole-making process from the lowest level of space-time to the highest complications of human life, a process that veils God while it yet intimates him.

The more general operation of divine Reality, in every area of the creation, is largely in terms of *incognitos*. Hence the beauty and truth men love, the goodness they discern in others, the ideals to which they devote their lives, and the demands they feel laid upon them are ways in which the divine Reality makes himself known and effects his purpose in one or another individual or group, and by one or another mode. He has set laws for the world; but he himself is present in these laws. He is not one who gave them and went away, but one who is their immanent and present life. So we can trace something of his working throughout the universe; we can see him in every area of life, both personal and social; we can recognize that the rise and fall of nations is according to his plan, as these peoples conform or fail to conform to his will; and we can also see

that individuals achieve or fail to achieve relatively balanced and integrated personalities, as they are or are
not adjusted to Reality in whatever guise and under
whatever form he may have appeared to them for their
greater good.

Now it will be apparent that such a faith is at odds
with a whole set of our common assumptions. For we in
America have assumed that man is pretty much his own
lord and ruler; we have not taken account of human
dependence and the limited extent of our freedom. The
God who is Lord of history and the supreme Ruler of
life cuts across our sense of achievement, our belief in
our own human competence, our expediencies and
pragmatisms and relativisms. If there be God at all, he
cannot be accommodated to our little schemes, as if he
were a kind of 'Cosmic Companion' upon whom we
might call if we saw fit; he is the final authority and to
him belongs the final word. This sense of the deity of
God is being recovered for us by the 'new orthodoxy,'
and is all to the good. On the other hand, 'liberalism'
rightly maintained the warm intimacy of God's presence with man, his close relationship with us and his
pervasive activity in every range of life, so that he is
unescapable in his presence with us. But in dynamic
orthodoxy the immanence of God is declared as strongly
as his transcendence, for both are genuine parts of the
Christian picture.

The second affirmation of dynamic orthodoxy concerns man. Man is the creature of God and hence, by
definition, limited and finite; he cannot rightly pretend to be anything other than this. Yet he does so pre-

tend, and by that fact he becomes a sinner. Nor is this sin only an individual offense; it is also a socially conveyed *situation* in which men find themselves. The doctrines of the 'fall' and 'original sin' point mythically to the real truth about human nature. Man is created with capacities and potentialities that make it possible for him to grow into free and open communion in grace with his divine Creator; but, as a matter of fact, he is in rebellion against God so that the capacities and potentialities that should be used to relate him to God are used for his own personal satisfaction and in the end can lead only to disintegration of his personality, unless once again they are related to God himself. This means that man is both good and bad. He is good in his intended fulfilment; he is bad in his existential perversion of that end. He is a creature of God, and so good; he is a sinner who has denied his high calling, and so bad.

Man is a hylomorphic being in a hylomorphic universe. This word is not familiar to the common man but the facts it describes are entirely familiar. Man and the universe are a union of matter and form, of physical stuff and spiritual stuff, so that it is absurd and self-defeating to try to interpret man or world in terms of matter alone or in terms of spirit alone. In religious language, the world and man are both sacramental in nature—that is, matter is being used to express spirit, one thing is at work in and through another. Man's body relates him to the whole flux and flow of the created order; his spirit relates him more directly to the divine Reality— he is an amphibian, living in an amphibious world.

Because this is true, Christianity is necessarily concerned not simply about saving men's souls, but also
about helping their bodies. It cannot abstract one from
the other: what God has here joined together, no man
can put asunder.

Given this total account of man as body-soul or soul-
body, as good by creation yet sinner by choice, Christianity can understand the tragedy of our existence; to
use Pascal's words, it can see both the 'misery' and the
'grandeur' of man. As against the common view of
Americans today, there is depth and reach in the Christian understanding of human nature and its dilemma.
Whereas we commonly tend to think that a little more
education, a little more good will, or a little more cleverness will suffice to get us out of any difficulty, Christianity sees that this is merely self-deception. Man is in
too serious a situation, his life too tangled, his world too
much the reflection of his own distortions, to admit of
any simple solution of his problems. Kierkegaard spoke
of *angst*—the dread and awe and fear about life and its
destiny, which men know now and again and can never
deny, try as they may. This is so much at the heart of
Christian insight that it can face and accept the depths
to which man can fall as well as the heights to which
he can rise.

At the same time the Christian faith indicates that
even in the planned society human nature will remain
human nature and the fundamental human situation
will be unchanged. If we suppose, as we do suppose,
that the new order in America will be democratic and
liberal, with extended rights and privileges for all its

citizens, we are to remember that in it men will yet be souls with bodies, bodies with souls, bound to the flux and flow of matter and yet moving upward to contemplate the realm of spirit. They will yet be sinners, conscious of defection from the possible good. They will yet be disappointed, frustrated victims of their own fears and their own failures. They will yet suffer and see others suffer; they will die and they will know bereavement in the death of others. This world's goods will never suffice them; and the neatest of utopias will still leave them ultimately unsatisfied, for they are not created to be 'contented pigs' but to be 'sons of God.'

A third central affirmation of Christian faith is that the eternal and loving Reality has taken action in history for man the finite, sinful creature. While God has never left himself without witness; while he has constantly been moving in and through his world, informing it with his purpose and conforming it to his will; while he is the *ground* of every human life, acting in it and through it, as through the rest of the world, but in a peculiarly intimate manner; while in every area of human experience he is known either outright or through one of his incognitos; while he has done and is doing all this, yet he has done still more. In the historical fact which we call Jesus Christ, he has entered uniquely and decisively into human life, taking one instance of that humanity for his special instrument. Under the conditions of a full and genuine human existence in a particular time and place, he has dwelt as Man. In so doing, he both has revealed the nature and purpose of God for man and has poured into humanity a new stream of life-giving power, into contact with which men are drawn and thereby raised to the level of his own unique life. Thus he dwells in them and they in him; and through this total process, which began with his coming and has gone on through his human life and death and resurrection, sinful man is reintegrated into the divine purpose and finds a fulfilment of life that begins in this world and carries the promise of eternity. The Incarnation and Atonement are at the heart of all Christian faith.

These doctrines are not merely historic fact; they are a continuing and present one, for the significance of the Christian Church is that it is the continuing of the Body of Christ, although now in social terms. We need not dwell on this point, for we sketched it at the beginning of the last chapter. The Church is linked with the Incarnation and the Atonement. And with the Church, there comes the doctrine of the Holy Spirit, whose work of response to God's action through the entire created world is concentrated significantly in the Body of Christ, where that response is intensified as God's action towards his world has on its side been intensified.

Once again, this faith both corrects and completes the assumptions of secular man. For it tells him that if he is to be saved at all, he must be saved by something other than his own efforts. Yet it tells him that he is good enough for God to bother about; his pride of place is wrong, but his insistence that he has worth is right. Dynamic orthodoxy introduces into the heart of our secular existence a new principle, the divine-human life of Christ, dwelling in the world and working out into the world through men and women set in the secular sphere. It makes it plain that human life requires fulfilment from outside and it presents the means to that fulfilment in a divine society composed of men and women whose only claim is that they have been drawn into the fellowship of Christ their Saviour. It introduces a divine society in which the very thing that a social order cannot do is in fact being done. The impartation of sense of human dignity in the cosmos, the ordering of human life in the sight of eternal truth, the redemption of men from frustration and from sin: these are accomplished in the Church. No secular society can even hope to accomplish them.

Finally, dynamic orthodoxy declares that man has a 'hope of glory'—and contrariwise, that he may 'perish everlastingly.' It asserts that this world is not all that matters, thus contradicting one of the major assumptions of our time. Yet it goes on to say that this world is vitally important, for it is here that the determination of ultimate destiny is made. It says that man may begin here to make himself a partaker of his fruition in God, which is heaven; on the other hand, he may so reject all that tends toward his good that he is doomed to lose God, which is to lose all that makes life ultimately significant. Nor is this Christian eschatology confined to the souls of men alone. It includes their bodies, in that it insists that their bodies play a part in their total personality, and that, in the conclusion of the matter, they will continue to play a part, although in a manner appropriate to the heavenly sphere. It includes also the whole created order, from the lowest levels to the highest, affirming that in some fashion, which God alone can know, the entire creation will take its proper place and have its proper part in the consummation. The doctrine of the resurrection of the body, so held, has a richness and depth that far exceed any assertion of immortality or the 'indestructibility of the soul.'

Perhaps what has been written will make clear that this dynamic orthodoxy avoids the excesses of 'liberalism' and the 'new orthodoxy' of our own day, and that it has its message to the secular world of our time, both in its cultural aspects and in its political and social embodiments. This kind of orthodoxy is entirely hospitable to whatever new truth may come from any direction; it is not the kind of orthodoxy Erasmus once described, that took 'the new learning to be synonymous with heresy,' and so made 'orthodoxy synonymous with ignorance.' Yet it is directly in line with the faith of the ancient Church and with the great theologians of the past.

It shares with that faith and with those theologians a recognition of still another fact, to which we must give a little space. That is the tension that must always exist in human life, between the eternal loyalties that belong to God alone and the temporal loyalties that are due to mundane society. A sheer 'otherworldliness' would deny the claims of this present existence; a sheer 'this-worldliness' would deny the claims of eternity. Man lives in both realms, of eternity and of time, precisely as he lives in the two realms of matter and spirit. This is the explanation of that discontent he carries with him wherever he goes. A man who does not have this sense of 'the more' that makes its demands upon him is not a true man; neither is the man who lives so much 'in the spirit' that he fails to notice he has a body, and thereby commits what M. Maritain has termed 'the fallacy of angelism.'

It is similar with regard to our cultural situation. If we are men, we must live in a culture that is 'of this world.' If we are men, we must make terms with the demands of the infinite upon us. If we are Christian men, we must live not only in a culture that is 'of this world,' but also in a culture that is 'of heaven.' For if a culture means a whole orientation of life, with its standards and ways of acting, with its total outlook, the Christian Church is precisely that. And by participation in the Church, the Christian has the specifically Christian 'culture' inbred in him. As Christians, then, we are amphibians in still another sense; we are both *of* the Church and *of* secular society.

We have said that the common assumptions of our American culture are either non-Christian or imperfectly Christian, in origin and in form. We have said that the new society, governed by these assumptions, will introduce control and planning that will diminish personal freedom while they promote larger social good. But the Christian is one who has a set of assumptions different from those of secular culture, and he is one who lives in a society that seeks none other than God himself. The Christian, then, must base his life on the fact of God and his revealed will for man. He can never

accept the notion that expediency alone is the guide to
behavior, nor can he be contented with a conception of
truth that in essence makes it dependent upon workability. His 'pragmatism' is of a very different kind from
that which flourishes in our schools and universities and
has permeated the popular mind. The Christian cannot believe that, in view of the imperfect nature of our
apprehension of ultimates, behavior as well as thinking
is to be judged in terms of 'relativism,' nor can he con-
cur in the popular notion that religious faith is only a
matter of taste or opinion. What he describes as 'self-
expression' is not the prevalent meaning of that phrase.
And his view of human life is never confined to this
world, for he believes in the eternal destiny of man
and the cosmic implications of all that he is and all
that he does.

Hence the Christian will find that in his daily con-
duct he is bound to bring into the picture values and
standards far removed from those commonly accepted
by his fellow citizens. To take some simple illustrations,
he will bring to his reading of current novels a set of
principles different from those of the conventional
reader. He will look at political movements, the need
for social improvement and reform, with a different
orientation from that of the ordinary 'man of good
will.' If he is in business, he will be concerned that
Christian assumptions about human relationships find
expression there; if he is a professional man, he will regard his work with all the devotion involved in a 'vocation' to which he has been summoned by God for the
service of his fellowmen.

Yet the Christian must live in the world of men, he must make his living, and he must get along with those who do not share his point of view. It is not part of his life as a Christian to attempt to run away from the situation in which he finds himself; he must rather seek to do the best he can in that situation. At a recent conference on social and economic questions, one of the speakers delivered the sentiment that in a world such as ours today, the Christian must emulate the early Christians and be prepared to 'flee to the mountains.' Another member of the conference rose to ask one question, which he said, was asked 'for information only.' The question was, 'Where are the mountains?'

We must live in the world, even while we belong to the Church. We cannot completely evade the assumptions of the secular culture, although we may regard them as wrong. This is bound to create serious problems. The Christian who is in the world and participates in its affairs is sure to have tensions that will make life anything but simple: if he were in a monastery it might be different, although even there he would have problems of adjustment, for the cloister depends on the market-place in more ways than one.

To become a Christian is not to be given a simple solution of one's difficulties. It is, in certain ways, to be given even more problems that must be solved. The Incarnation or the Atonement does not give us answers to problems so much as it gives us a new insight into them and a new way of facing them. The ordinary Christian is given certain things: he has a new *altitude* above the world of affairs; he has a new *attitude* toward the problems he must face; and he has a new *aptitude* for handling life situations—namely, the grace of God in Christ which is reflected in charity toward men. But he still has the problems; and he must still live in a secular environment. If he fails to come to some kind of terms with that environment, he will simply destroy himself. If he accepts it completely, he will deny his Christian profession. Hence he must try to compromise.

Both the word and the idea of 'compromise' are very much disliked by many of our contemporary religious writers. Yet in some degree everyone does compromise; if life is to be a possibility at all, one must do so. The real danger in compromise comes if and when it is indulged in without understanding and without principle. Now in the process of adjustment to the world and its ways, the Christian must know what he is about; one of the real contributions the 'cell' can make to him personally is that it can keep him alive to his compromising, and give him the strength to maintain his firm Christian position and point of view, at the very time he is involved in secular assumptions that are not his own and is accepting by necessity a social situation that he believes imperfect. Further, the Christian Church itself through its theologians and moralists can be of enormous help to the practicing Christian in this connection. It can work out, for this time and for tomorrow, what we may flatly describe as a 'casuistry' by which life will be possible for the ordinary Christian man or woman. Failure to do this has been responsible for a large measure of the confusion and the uncertainty of the earnest Christian who needs guidance, but who looks for it in vain.

The tendency has been for Christian moralists to 'talk big' in terms of ideals and goals, but to be silent when concrete questions are asked. We are told that 'Christian ideals' are to govern our behavior; yet that means we are simply given some end but are not helped to reach it from where we are. Or, in answer to our problem, we are taught that it is the Christian's duty to be a loyal churchman, performing his particular religious obligations, such as church-going and the like, saying his prayers, contributing to the Church and to philanthropic organizations. But that solution only makes religion a special field with little or no relation to the exigencies of daily life apart from the specifically religious. What we need is a study of the issues of contemporary life as men must live it, in the light of the eternal truths that Christianity believes have been revealed by God. And on that basis, we need some practical principles that will enable us to see how we can do what we have to do, with as good a conscience as possible, with a minimum of compromise, and with a willed effort to bring as much of eternal truth into immediate practice as is possible under given circumstances.

To take a single instance, the businessman needs help in working out a business ethic that is not simply the conventionally accepted one, but that has been developed in the light of the Christian insistence on honesty, integrity, justice, and the rights of one's brothers to their share in the world's goods. Or again, the physician and the lawyer need a practical ethic that will help them to see what Christianity means in their callings. In many fields something of this sort is done personally by the Christian businessman or the physician or the lawyer; but they are doing it alone and in a hit-or-miss fashion, because the Christian Church has no moral theology and casuistry that will be of use to them. The traditional system, found in the Roman Catholic Church, is outworn; yet such a moral theology, based on dynamic orthodoxy and expressed in modern language, is vitally necessary for us all today and will be even more necessary tomorrow.

The one place where this kind of job has been done is in relation to social movements and the economic development of the new society. Here we have had the benefit of sound thinking, and the Christian who is not a mere reactionary on the one hand nor a sheer visionary on the other can discover guidance that will help him in his search for the right movements to support and the right causes to sponsor. But in almost every other area he feels helpless.

Once again we can turn to the sexual morality of youth for an illustration. The typical American notions about human life and destiny are clearly at work in the realm of sexual behavior, and the young Christian is often sadly perplexed and worried. He probably accepts the Christian assumptions, so far as he knows them, but conforms to the usual social norms. He has had little or no guidance from the Church, beyond mere prohibition and condemnation. It is common knowledge that this has not been very effective, even among the most devoted of the Christian youth of the land. In effect, their behavior does not differ markedly from that of their non-Christian fellows. Expediency, pragmatism, relativity, and the like would seem to say one thing; but does the Christian have anything more or anything different to say about it? It requires slight experience as a parish priest or a minister, if one has had the confidence of young people in this intimate problem, to know that they will welcome guidance and try to follow it, if only it is based on some really sound standards and commends itself as congruous with their faith and possible in their actual life-situation.

Or take the use of contraceptives. Evidently all Christian bodies, excepting the Roman Catholic Church (and that is a doubtful exception, in view of the approval given the 'rhythm theory' and the right of limitation of sexual intercourse to 'safe periods'), are willing to accept the practice. But with what limits and safeguards? Is wholesale approval a Christian attitude, if wholesale condemnation is not? Upon what is the Christian attitude to be based? It can only be based upon something like natural law, whose meaning must be extended in the light of our revised conception of man and his place in the world, our deepened knowledge of psychology and physiology, and our consideration of sociological as well as economic factors. But apart from a few scattered pronouncements, the whole matter has been left up in the air, and the average Christian is not guided in this vital matter by the results of careful and thoughtful study in the light of the total Christian position.

If the Christian Church, with its affirmations about God, Man, and the redemption of human nature, and its convictions concerning the destiny that awaits us and our world, is to play its part not only in the making of a new world, but also among the actual members of the Church itself, it must face these questions, and others like them, and reach conclusions.

In the areas to which we have been referring, almost nothing has been done. In fact, the writer can recall only a little essay by Dr. Leonard Hodgson, containing his inaugural lecture as Regius Professor of Moral Theology at Oxford, in which he argued vigorously for such a study as we ourselves have demanded, and insisted that the Church must produce, within as short a time as possible, some simple and helpful books that will be available to Christian people who are urgently seeking guidance. In America this may have been discussed at conferences and by theologians and moralists; it has so far given us very little in the way of concrete results. In the past, an application of the eternal Christian principles and of the natural law, as the Church saw them, to the given situations in which men found themselves, was always a part of the total Christian theology; it ought to be so today. In the light of the vastly changed cultural scene, with our new knowledge, our technical equipment, our mechanized world, our sociological sense, the Christian moral imperative must speak meaningfully and helpfully to the man or woman who wishes to be a Christian even while he must at the same time earn his living, be a citizen, share in the affairs of secular life, and take his place in the world of men.

A moral theology with its expression in a 'casuistry' for the average man would not be easy to create; nor would it be final and complete. It would be a growing and changing thing, but it would at any rate take account of the facts and not leave the individual Christian stranded. Indeed, if such a moral theology were developed, on the basis of a dynamic orthodoxy true to historic Christianity but not afraid of the new facts that have come to us and the new situations in which we live, we may venture to think that many of the harmful tensions would disappear, at least as a *hidden* disease. Instead, we should have healthy because recognized tensions in loyalties with which men could deal to some degree, because they knew where the tensions were and what they were about.

The Christian lives by faith, hope, and charity. He lives by faith in God, not in men, although his faith in God is reflected in his trust that there is a goodness in human nature that is the image of God himself; he lives by the hope not that *his* ideas of what ought to be shall be realized, but in the confident expectation that God's will shall be done; he lives by charity, in that commitment to God's goodness which is reflected in a growing awareness of the divine Reality and a growing sensitivity to men and their need. Hence he is enabled to *live*, not to exist; and he is able, like the Southern Negress, 'to wear this world like a loose garment.' He can be careless, because he knows that God cares; he can care deeply, because God's caring shines through him, and through him reaches out to touch all life and all men. This is the secret of Christianity, manifested in the saints and in 'humble men of heart'; and it is by this that the Christian is enabled to share in 'the victory that overcometh the world.' 'Be of good cheer,' said our Lord as the Fourth Gospel reports, 'I have overcome the world.' But before those words, he had said, 'In the world ye shall have tribulation.'

That means, we may say, that superficial ease and comfort are not for the Christian to expect. Miguel de Unamuno, in his *Tragic Sense of Life*, writes, 'May God deny you peace, but grant you glory.' Peace in the cheap sense, bought at the price of surrender, is not worth having; glory, a share in God's own divine life, is our goal—and when we have that, we have indeed the real peace 'which passeth human understanding.'

It is this kind of life that is made possible by the Christian faith; it is this that is validated by the view of the world that we have called dynamic orthodoxy. Such a faith is as much needed by men today as it was yesterday; it will be their great need tomorrow. Men may come to see that the common assumptions of American culture are inadequate for any fully human life, since they minimize or neglect so much that is intrinsic to it. When men see this, they may once again wish to have the eternal reality of God as their resource, his will for men as their guide to true human living, his power as their strength. In the new society, where personal expression will be more and more difficult as the state takes over more and more areas of life, men may once again wish to have some refuge, as it were, where they may be *themselves*. In any case, they will need help and guidance in living as free men in a society that, even if for their good, limits the area of choice and initiative. And because they are men, they will always have a desire—perhaps hidden in the depths of their being—for some firm anchorage that can give them inner poise and sense of meaning, as they face life's vicissitudes and know the suffering and pain, the happiness and joy, the 'changes and chances' of this world. But if there is to be any faith that commends itself to men, it must be able to appreciate the goods they know in their secular experience, the truths they have discovered, the beauty they have created, the simple pleasures of secular life. It must not be arrogant and superior, but must be able somehow to relate all that is good and right to the supreme reality of God. It is because the faith of the Christian centuries has been able to do just this, when it has been alive and alert and aware of its own nature, that we can feel confident of the abiding value of dynamic orthodoxy, even though we accept it *not* because it 'works,' but because to our enlighted thinking and our deepest pondering it is known to be *true*.

We are, then, by no means hopeless about the Christian faith in the present situation or in the world of tomorrow. Nor are we hopeless about the Christian Church. 'Man's extremity is God's opportunity'; the hour when we seem least able to find our way is the hour when we are called to greater trust and firmer faith. It is in such a spirit that we ought to face the future, knowing that in the changed world of our time the gospel remains God's message of salvation; and that in the new society that will be ours tomorrow that gospel and the Church which proclaims it will still be what they have been since the day of Pentecost: the means by which God, through his Holy Spirit, will 'direct and rule us, according to [his] will, comfort us in all our afflictions, defend us from all error, and lead us into all truth.' There need be no fear that the day will come when the gospel will be irrelevant to man in his need, when the Christian Church as the carrier of that gospel will not have its God-given place.

What is needed above all today, and what will be needed even more tomorrow, is a heightened self-consciousness or self-awareness among Christians. We do not mean a priggishness or a hypocritical pretension to be what we are not. We mean an awareness of the privilege of Christian discipleship, of the obligations that discipleship lays upon the believer as well as of the opportunities it offers him. We mean a consciousness of the fact that one *is* a Christian, called to a peculiar kind of life and a unique loyalty to the divine imperative. We mean a developing sense of the rich significance of belonging to the Body of Christ, as a member of that Body through whom its life—the life of God-made-Man—flows freely. We mean that 'the Church must *become* the Church,' must seek to realize what in God's purpose it already is; and that those who are its members must likewise realize, so far as they are able by the help of the Holy Spirit, the fact of their new nature as partakers of the divine life through Christ. With this accomplished, the Church will stand firm in the changing world, providing a beacon light and a place of refuge for the sons of men.

As never before in Christian history since the days of

the Roman Empire, the Christian Church is called to
be both the ark of salvation, in that it gives to men the
certainty of life in God, and the continuing agent of
redemption, in that from it and through it health-giving influences stream out into the whole world. All too
often the former of these has been emphasized to the
neglect of the latter. But the Church is both; its very
nature as the Body of Christ should make that plain.
Christ's mission among us was both to bring the salvation of God to the little company of followers whom
he called to be with him, and also, through them, to
leaven the world with his divine life.

As to the final result, it is not for us 'to know the times
nor the seasons, which the Father hath put in his own
authority.' The only thing we know, and all we need to
know, is that we have been made witnesses of Christ
and bearers of the Spirit's power, 'both in Jerusalem,
and in all Judaea, and in Samaria, and unto the utter-
most part of the earth.' The conclusion of the matter,
therefore, is that we are called to be Christians in any
society and under any conditions, so that 'God in all
things may be glorified through Jesus Christ, to whom
be praise and dominion for ever and ever. Amen.'